John Lord Hayes

The Protective Question Abroad

John Lord Hayes

The Protective Question Abroad

ISBN/EAN: 9783744694278

Printed in Europe, USA, Canada, Australia, Japan

Cover: Foto ©ninafisch / pixelio.de

More available books at **www.hansebooks.com**

THE

PROTECTIVE QUESTION ABROAD,

AND

𝕽emarks at the 𝕴ndianapolis 𝕰xposition.

By JOHN L. HAYES.

FROM THE BULLETIN OF THE NATIONAL ASSOCIATION OF
WOOL MANUFACTURERS.

CAMBRIDGE:
PRESS OF JOHN WILSON AND SON.
1870.

PROTECTIVE QUESTION ABROAD.

It cannot be denied that a tendency to free-trade doctrine largely prevails in our great cities, in fashionable circles, and among literary and professional men, and, what is more than all to be regretted, in our colleges. To the importing merchants and agents of foreign houses, and to the newspapers who depend upon them for advertisements, free trade is merely a personal question of livelihood. To people of fashion it recommends itself by a meaner motive. When the tariff was under discussion in 1867, the prince of American dry-goods importers, at a public reception in Washington, gathered about him a circle of fashionable women, and readily made them converts to his doctrine, by asserting that, if the pending tariff bill should pass, their silks would cost a dollar a yard more. Many professional and literary men, with scarcely a broader scan, see in the protective system only the cause of the increased prices of labor, and hence of their necessities. But the influence, of all others, which sways the mind, or rather what assumes to be the mind, of the country towards free trade, which warps the press, and is irresistible in the college, is the idea so carefully inculcated by the propagandists of free trade, that their doctrines are sanctioned by all the intellect of Europe. Free trade is thus accepted, like the last Paris fashion, or is assumed as the young men of the clubs assume certain manners, because "it is English, you know."

But foreign opinion, or the experience of other nations having conditions of existence analogous to our own, cannot, any more

than the lessons of history, be lightly regarded by the philosopher or statesman. If it be true, as is arrogantly asserted, that
" to relax commercial systems, and not to restrict them, is alone
in accordance with the spirit of the age," * and that "the leading
commercial nations, the United States alone excepted, have
been relaxing of late years their commercial systems," a public opinion abroad, although no conclusive argument against
the protective policy here, would be a reason for questioning
it. The assertion, however, we believe to be wholly unsupported
by examples, with the single exception of England. Of Russia
it is declared in the official reports of English Chambers of Commerce, " that the importation of manufactured tissues is practically prevented, by a scale of duties higher than any in the
world." Some concession was made to Great Britain in 1869 ;
but is admitted to be but a very slight measure of free trade,
which " would not lead to an extension of legitimate trade, although it might make smuggling less profitable." The Austrian
tariff is characterized by the same English authority as " present-
ing features of the most objectionable character, while the duties
are almost prohibitory." This was said in 1865. Recent changes
still leave the average duties on fabrics in Austria from 24 to
67 per cent.† The Swedish tariff is referred to as having " the

---

* Professor Perry.

† Mr. Behrens, President of the Chamber of Commerce of Bradford, in
a speech at the annual meeting of the Association of Chambers of Commerce,
of the United Kingdom, February, 1869, said : —

" As to Austria, we had the same advantages as the most favored nations, by
virtue of a treaty which had received the sanction of the Reichsrath ; but there
was a supplementary convention, negotiated by Sir L. Mallet, which, unfortunately, had not yet received that sanction. It was entered, in order to carry out
the treaty, which provided that no specific duty should exceed twenty per cent
of the value of the imported goods ; and that after 1872 it should not exceed
fifteen per cent. Now, the protectionists in Austria were quite aghast at this ;
for, although they always used to say that the fixed duties agreed upon did not
amount to more than five or ten per cent, when pressed to allow a restriction to
fifteen per cent, they said it would be ruin to them.

" On Sir L. Mallet visiting Bradford, he put patterns before him, and showed
that the duties had averaged from twenty-four to sixty-seven per cent. He
hoped the exertions made by our government, and well seconded by the Austrian government, would have some result ; so that, even if we did not get our

unfortunate distinction of disputing with Spain the debatable honor of being the highest in the world, the Russian only excepted." The Peninsula is declared by British manufacturers to "be shut out from the products of the looms and forges of England by a most ridiculous tariff." The Anglo-French treaty is pronounced by Count Gasparin to be scarcely less prohibitory in fact than the Morrill tariff. This treaty, we admit, cannot be fairly cited as indicating either an affirmative or negative sentiment as to the protective question, on the part of the Imperial Government which concluded it. It would seem that the purpose of the Emperor was to conciliate England, by apparent concessions to her free-trade policy, while practically yielding as little as possible. Mr. Cobden and his friends claim the treaty as a free-trade victory. The Bradford Chamber of Commerce complains that the French tariff is still "excessive," "unreasonable," and "onerous." Whether it indicates a free-trade progress or not, the actual protective sentiment of France is shown by the arguments made for and against the commercial treaties. They are defended by the political supporters of the Govern-

---

full pound of flesh, we might obtain a good, practical treaty. As to Russia, the new tariff announced by Mr. Mitchell would not lead, he thought, to an extension of legitimate trade, at least as far as this country was concerned ; but it might make smuggling a little less profitable.

"In proof that it was not based on any intelligible principle, he might mention that yarns and machinery were actually subject to higher duties than previously, thus impeding the progress of Russian manufactures. It was said that the sole reason for the change was the desire to have a round sum instead of a fraction. While preaching free trade, however, to foreign nations, we must not forget our colonies, against which we had just ground of complaint. As long as they required the protection of the mother country, we might fairly demand that the leading principles of our policy should be accepted as fundamental. He presumed that no English colony would be allowed to introduce slavery, or arbitrary imprisonment, or any thing contrary to our fundamental principles. Now, surely free trade was one of those principles. What we asked foreign countries to adopt, we had a perfect right to require from our colonies. In newly peopled countries it might, perhaps, be right to enforce a duty on imports, as the only way of raising revenue ; but it should be limited to the purposes of revenue, and should not act as a protective duty. Some of the seaboard provinces of the Canadian Confederation used to have five, seven and one-half, or ten per cent duties; but one result of the Confederation had been to substitute a uniform duty of fifteen per cent."

ment, for the very reason that they are sufficiently protective
of French industry; and are opposed by the practical men of
France, for the reason that they have been disastrous to her
industries. M. Pouyer Qartier, eminent both as a manufacturer and statesman, in a speech before the Congress of the
learned societies of France during the present year, "com-
plained of the treaties of commerce of 1860, which had been
in operation ten years, and demanded what developments the
treaties had procured for French industry, and if agriculture
had derived any advantage from it. He separated himself from
the political economists (free traders), when they wished to apply
economical science to France. In England the strife was opened
by the manufacturers against the landed proprietors. In France
it was the men of doctrine who had taken the initiative. Hence
all our misfortunes. They had no experience, and hence they
could not fail to take the wrong roads." These remarks illus-
trate the truth which will be apparent to any one who reads the
French journals, that free trade is generally repudiated by the
practical men of France. It is supported by extreme or specu-
lative philosophers, and by sentimentalists of the liberal school,
like Jules Simon, who closes his late speech in the *Corps Législatif* with the transcendental argument : ("All the liberties are
sisters ; if we have liberty of trade, we shall have the others.")

Mr. Carey has shown that the shattered fragments which five
and thirty years ago passed with the world as Germany, united
into a German Confederation by the Zollverein, and with its
industry protected by a scale of duties which effectually disarmed
English competition, then bearing down all the industry of Europe,
entered through the gates of the protective policy upon the career
which has had so brilliant a culmination. The new policy secured
a market on the land for nearly all its products, and, as a necessary
consequence, an agricultural population which grows daily both in
intelligence and power. Thirteen years ago Mr. Carey expressed
the opinion that Germany, " whose national sin for two centuries
has been poverty," already stood first in Europe in point of intel-
lectual development, and was advancing in the physical and moral
condition of her people with a rapidity exceeding that of any

portion of the eastern hemisphere. The philosopher is the only seer. How marvellously are these predictions confirmed by the events which now startle the world! To what, says Mr. Carey, is the progress due? ("To the great and simple operations of the protective features of the system of the Zollverein, long regarded by me as the most important measure of the century, and among the most important ever adopted in Europe.") We demand what really truly protective feature of the Zollverein duties has been modified in accordance with the spirit of the age? It is vain to say that the duties are low compared with our own, since they are carefully adjusted to the admitted and actual necessities of the manufactures which they are designed to protect. Low as the apparent rate of duties in the Zollverein, they are stated by Mr. Burn, of Manchester, in his recent pamphlet, to be "practically prohibitory" of British manufactured goods. It does not affect the question whether the duties are 50 or 5 per cent, if the lower duty act equally for the advantage of the industry of the country which seeks to exclude injurious competition from abroad. A careful observation will show that all the boasted concessions to free trade in the continental tariffs, such as the admission of yarns, warps, and thrown-silk, which are of the nature of raw material, are made as measures of "qualified protection," of which we shall hereafter speak, and with the avowed object of encouraging native industries.* If any doubt existed

---

* The protective character of the Zollverein is confirmed by the following extract from a recent article by Mr. Henry Carey Baird : —

"To this grand result (the Zollverein) the two men, not in official position, who contributed most, were Frederic List and Baron Cotta. The central and controlling ideas of List, who was an eminent and popular political economist, were a nationality for his native land and the building up of a diversified industry by means of protection. These were the great ends he aimed at, and these thoughts can be traced on nearly every page of his 'National System of Political Economy,' from the title itself to the concluding line of the book. As to whether the tariff gave the protection required, as well as to the results of it, there can be no more competent authority than he. Of the tariff and its effects, writing in 1841, he says : —

"'We hesitate not to say it affords a protection from twenty to sixty per cent on manufactured goods;' and adds, 'Germany in the space of ten years has advanced a century in prosperity, in self-respect, and power. How so? The

as to the protective sentiment in Germany, it is set at rest by
the fact, that the works of our great protective philosopher have
been translated into the German and Italian languages, passed
through numerous editions, and adopted and studied as text-books
in continental universities.   If we add to these examples that of
India, whose finance minister, Mr. Wilson, long a free trader,
found that the adoption of measures tending towards protection
was the only means of saving the remaining manufactures of
that magnificent country, impoverished by the opposite policy;
that of Australia, which has already entered vigorously upon the
protective policy ; and that of Canada, which less vigorously, but
no less surely, is tending in the same direction, — what examples
remain to prove that the leading commercial nations are relaxing
their commercial systems?   The example of England alone.

SIR EDWARD SULLIVAN AND ENGLAND.

Among the many recent indications that a change of opinion as
to the working of the free-trade system is going on now in England, the most important is the work recently published, entitled
"Protection to Native Industry," by Sir Edward Sullivan,
Baronet, author of "Ten Chapters on Social Reform ;" the re-
publication of which, in this country, we owe to Mr. H. C. Baird,
of Philadelphia, and the Bureau Printing Company of Chicago.
Sir Edward occupies a respectable place in the magistracy
of his country, being a justice of the peace and deputy-lieutenant
of the County of Lancaster.   His father was an admiral of the
Blue, and his family is traced back to one of the kings of
Munster.   The testimony of one occupying the social position of
this writer is particularly valuable, as it assures us that he has
no bias for the industrial class which he seeks to relieve, while

---

suppression of the barriers and custom-houses which separated the German
States has been an excellent measure; but it had borne bitter fruit if home
industry had been exposed to foreign competition.   The protection of the tariff
of the Customs Union (Zollverein) extended to manufactured products in general
use has accomplished this wonderful change.' " (See Pol. Econ., Am. ed., p. 459.)

entirely independent of the commercial class, which derives the principal advantages from free trade in England. The author makes no pretension to philosophy or learning. He gives hardly a quotation, except from General Grant's inaugural; does not attempt to fortify himself with tables or statistics; does not accumulate facts, and even repeats such as he has collected. But his work is no less convincing, because it is the utterance of deep convictions. He is not deeply read in the doctrines of protection, and makes admissions which a closer reasoner would not do. But the book is the plain talk of a man of good practical sense, who utterly discards theory, and addresses himself to the facts before him; not in book language, but just as one man of the world talks with another; and with a freedom of expression which is not often found without flippancy.

Sir Edward, above all, wins our admiration by his defiance of the prejudice of his class, in boldly breaking a lance for the cause of the crushed working-men of England. It is a chivalric deed, not less knightly than the legendary feats of Sir Launcelot and the companions of the Round Table, when they went forth to free the English soil from oppressors in the "true old times,"

"When every morning brought a noble chance,
And every chance brought out a noble knight."

Our object is not to review, criticise, or even to condense this book, nor to make it a text for our commentaries. We shall serve our purpose, and more interest our readers who have not the work in their hands, by largely extracting such portions as show the new and unexpected phase of opinion in England as to a question upon which there has before been no divided sentiment.

The author states the purpose of his work with admirable simplicity and directness.

"Protection to native industry is not a question of sentiment or theory, but of fact and common sense. There is no magic or mystery about it; it is an ordinary calculation of cost, in which all the conditions and figures are perfectly well known. Wages in France, Belgium, Prussia, Austria, and in Switzerland, are from thirty to fifty per cent lower than in England : rent, clothing, food, beer, taxes, and general charges, are all in the same proportion. The habits of the people are economical in the extreme; the manufacturers have as much capital, science, and enterprise, and their operatives as much skill and intelligence, and technical education, and industry, as we have ; they get their raw materials very nearly at the same price we do. The question is, Can our manufacturers, with higher wages, higher rates and taxes, higher general charges, and our operatives, with dearer food, dearer clothing, dearer house-rent, and extravagant habits, produce as cheaply as they can ?

"The remedy for the present state of things is not to export our workmen and import our manufacturers, but to keep our workmen and manufacture for ourselves.

"England is the only country in the world that does not, in some shape or other, protect native industry, and preserve a preferential market for its own operatives. Theoretically, it may be very chivalrous: practically, it is very stupid, — c'est beau, mais c'est bête."

The author commences his treatise with a sensible chapter on the "Growth of Trade." He shows that at the very time, about twenty years since, when the gold of Australia and California, and the spread of steam communication by land and sea over the whole face of the globe, increased to an inconceivable extent the trade of the world, and equalized the trading conditions of the different nations, the Manchester School of Political Economists took out their patent, as it were, for free trade.

"They maintained their patent was so grand, and its advantages so evident, that every nation must adopt it, and that those who did so first would be the greatest gainers: so eager were they to begin, that, like most other things done in a hurry, it was only half done. To try the experiment at all, other nations must be found to join us ; to know what the result of free trade actually was, there must be reciprocity and free ports : but as no other nation joined us, we never had either one or the other. As we advanced, they drew back ; consequently, the experiment has never been tried, and we know to-day as little of free trade, strictly speaking, as we did twenty years ago. It is amusing to hear people expatiating on the marvels of free trade, and on the blessings it has conferred upon the human race in general, and ourselves in particular, when we remember that as yet this policy has never even been tried, that its miracles and blessings are still in

the womb of the future. Free traders renounce all logic and facts
when discussing their favorite dogma : they are, indeed, the most dis-
ingenuous of arguers. I declare, that, as constantly as I have heard
the subject discussed, I never once heard a free trader have the
honesty to attribute the increased trade of the world in general, and
of England as part of it, to its true causes, viz., the vast increase in
the circulating medium and the general application of steam, but
always to what they choose to call free trade. To ignore these illimit-
able agencies, and to ascribe all progress to the pigmy efforts of a
small school of political economists in England, is to reverse the old
proverb, and to imagine the mouse bringing forth the mountain.

"The increased foreign commerce of England, during the last
twenty years, is attributed to her free trade policy ; and we are led,
by implication, to understand that she is the only nation that has
advanced in commercial activity during that period ; that whilst she
has been advancing, the rest of the world has stood still.

"Free traders point with triumph to our Board of Trade returns
of exports and imports, and exclaim, triumphantly, This is our doing ;
but they ignore the fact — it cannot be through ignorance — that the
Board of Trade returns in France, Switzerland, Prussia, Belgium,
and Austria, show results far more satisfactory, a proportionate
increase of trade far exceeding our own.

"It is not England alone that has increased her trade during the
last twenty years : the whole of Europe and America, with some
trifling exceptions, have increased theirs far more rapidly than we
have. Take France, for instance, as being our nearest neighbor, and
compare her wealth and commercial position now with what it was
twenty years ago, and it will at once be granted that, however great
may be the blessings of free trade, sound progress is not incompatible
with the strictest protection ; and the bullion in the Bank of France
is now, in 1869, forty-seven millions, — twenty-seven millions higher
than it was in 1844, and sixteen millions higher than in 1853 : the
bullion in the Bank of England is seventeen millions, — two millions
higher than in 1844, three millions less than in 1853 !

"In France, in 1868, the exports and imports balanced within
twenty millions. In England, the excess of imports was over sixty
millions ! and in 1869 it will, in all probability, reach one hundred
millions.

"The increased commerce of the world has been caused by the
increased circulation of gold and the increased facilities of communication by land and sea : it never has been and never can be affected

THE PROTECTIVE QUESTION ABROAD.

by paltry legislation, either in one direction or the other. Local legislation, like that which has made England a free port, may affect the trade of England, but to suppose it will materially influence the commerce of the world would be preposterous; it is only our national bumptiousness that renders the idea possible. All the nations of the world have increased their commerce, — they under the strictest principle of protection, we alone under what we call free trade. [To attribute our progress to free trade is just as absurd as to attribute theirs to protection.] It might be more fairly said, we have all progressed in spite of both. Neither system has had more than an infinitesimal effect by the side of the great agencies that have brought about this result."

Similar views, but more condensely stated, had been before expressed by Mr. Bigelow in his Tariff Question, which evidently had not been seen by Sir Edward Sullivan. It is instructive to observe how these two writers corroborate each other.

After giving tables exhibiting the increase of British exports, Mr. Bigelow says: —

/ "The chief causes of this large increase of British exports are undoubtedly to be found outside of the tariff laws. That they are causes of general application, is shown by the fact, that Great Britain was not alone in this experience of prosperity. The foreign trade of France, under a tariff highly protective, increased, during the same period, in a ratio greater than that of England; and the United States, with a tariff moderately protective, had a commercial record equally advantageous, — as may be seen by the following comparative statement: —

Countries Compared.	Exports in 1853.	Exports in 1859.	Percentage of Increase.
	Dollars.	Dollars.	Per cent.
Great Britain	494,668,905	652,057,355	31.82
France	253,425,000	371,628,000	46.64
United States	189,869,162	278,392,080	46.62

"In accounting for this recent and great expansion of commerce, two causes especially suggest themselves: —

"*First*, The influence of applied sciences in augmenting the means of production; an influence which is constantly becoming more extensive and efficient.

" *Secondly,* The greatly increased supply of gold.

" This is pre-eminently an age of progress. Useful inventions in the mechanic arts, and important discoveries in science, are of almost daily occurrence. Countless improvements in existing machines, and in the methods and processes of production, are continually enlarging the ability to produce, — multiplying articles of consumption, and thus, of necessity, swelling the great currents of trade.

" The annual produce of gold, which, prior to 1848, was $50,000,000, has, since 1853, amounted to nearly $150,000,000. ' The effect of this treble supply of gold,' says Mr. Tooke, ' has been to set in motion and sustain a vast and increasing number of causes, all conducing to augment the real wealth and resources of the world, by stimulating trade, enterprise, discovery, and production.'

" While these are causes of general application, which operate with more or less effect in all commercial countries, there can be no doubt that they exert a peculiar power in England. This is an advantage which she owes to her superior capital and skill, and to her well-established system of production, and her widely extended business relations. These enable her to apply, readily and efficiently, to her productive means, every new improvement, and to meet with promptness every new demand; while under the all-controlling laws of commercial attraction, her position, as manufacturer for half the globe, draws to her vaults the larger part of the gold."

These views are confirmed by McCulloch, who says, in his Dictionary, edition of 1859 : —

" It would be difficult to exaggerate the advance that has been made in commerce, and in most sorts of industry, and the improvement in the condition of society that has taken place, during the last seven years. A considerable portion of this advance is no doubt due to the discovery of the Californian and Australian gold-fields."

The same causes had increased the manufactures and exports of England during the most brilliant period of her older commercial history. In the sixth and seventh years of Elizabeth, the woollen manufacture of England had so much increased, that the export of woollen goods to Antwerp alone, according to Camden, amounted to £750,000; and the whole value of the exports, in 1564, was £1,200,000, — all fabricated from English wool. The vigor of the woollen trade, the only textile

manufacture then established in England, is attributed by
Smith, a very high authority, in his celebrated memoirs of wool,
to *the abundance of gold and silver*, in consequence of the recent
discovery of South America.

In the chapter on free trade and free ports, Sir Edward Sullivan exposes the absurdity of the first canon of free trade, that
"each nation should supply to the world's market what it produces best and cheapest, and should resign to other nations those
industries in which it is not so strong." He observes, that it
would not be difficult to prove, that as capital and science
become more general, and the natural resources of different
countries are more fully developed, there will be scarcely a
single article of manufacture that will not be produced as
cheap by some one nation or other, as in England. And
he pertinently inquires: "If this ever takes place, even par-
tially, is England to sacrifice her existence to her theory, and
abandon all, or a portion of her industries, because she cannot
produce quite so cheaply as her neighbors? Is she to sink into
the position of a manufacturing country absolutely without
manufactures?"

He proceeds to show what are the actual results to the work-
people of England, with dear food, dear clothing, dear house-
rent, and a double rate of wages, of unrelieved competition,
with the work-people of other nations, whose superior advantages, more economical and thrifty habits, and a fostering
home support, enable them to undersell the English. The distress of the English operatives, who have been pushed out of
their home market by foreign competition, is shown by the
increasing crime and pauperism of the country. "The pauperism and crime of the country," says Sir Edward, "are increasing
so rapidly, that we must look the difficulty in the face, and try
to mitigate it, or we must shut our eyes and ears, and let
destruction come upon us; at the rate they are now increasing,
this need not be very long. In the year 1853, fifteen years
ago, the amount expended in actual relief of the poor was
under five millions; in 1868 it was seven and a half millions,
an increase of fifty per cent in fifteen years. Nearly the whole

of this increase, and also the increase of crime, has been in the manufacturing districts." He continues : —

"The manufacturing districts are depressed as they never have been before; and any one who will visit them may see by evidence that cannot lie, by smokeless chimneys, by closed shops, by crowded poorhouses and glutted jails, by crowds of squalid idlers, that the distress is real. Take the one single fact that the consumption of cotton goods in England has fallen off 35 per cent in three years! Can any fact afford stronger proof of the poverty and depression of our operative classes ? Cotton constitutes the greater proportion of the clothing of the lower orders ; when, therefore, the consumption of cotton falls away, it is proof positive that the working classes are taking less clothing.

"Those who wish to learn the present condition of affairs must not consult the wealthy political leaders of the manufacturing districts, — men who have realized their wealth, and to a great extent have converted their workshops into farms. They are land-owners, not manufacturers, — consumers rather than producers, — and they can afford to see trade leaving their districts without danger or alarm.

"No : they must go amongst the workers, the managers, and active owners of manufactories, amongst men whose capital is still at stake, amongst the operatives, the small shopkeepers and householders who crowd the manufacturing districts. You do not hear so much of the present manufacturing depression at Manchester, where an immense proportion of the wealth is realized, invested in lands or in the 3 per cents, and where the fortunate owners have abandoned the struggling existence of trade for the more brilliant life of politics. It is amongst smaller men and less fortunate districts that the real suffering and distress is witnessed, — amongst the small and moderate capitalists still struggling, striving, disappointed. Manchester represents the past, not the present, condition of the manufacturing industries ; it is in Bolton, Wigan, Stockport, Oldham, Preston, Coventry, Nottingham, Macclesfield, not in Manchester, that the true tale of sorrow and ruin is heard. You must read the never-ending and still-increasing lists of failures and bankruptcies that decimate every trade and industry in the country. Never in the history of England has that portion of the commercial class, that depends on home consumption and home prosperity, been so depressed, despondent, and ruined ! Never has home consumption been at such a low ebb in every article consumed by the working classes. It is not cotton only that is depressed ; cotton is, comparatively, flourishing : it is every trade and every industry that is in the difficulties. Of this universal depression of industries I have no doubt whatever; it is only now, only within the last three years, that the foreign producers have acquired the skill and capital and machinery that enables them really to press us out of our own markets. The shadow has been coming over us for many years, but it is only just now we are beginning to feel the substance; their progress corresponds with our decline. A great manufacturing nation like England does not suddenly collapse and give place to another; her industries are slowly, bit by bit, replaced by those of other countries; the process is gradual, and we are undergoing it at present. The difference between England and her young manufacturing rivals is simple, but alarming. France, Austria, Prussia, Belgium, Switzerland, have increased their export trade and their home consumption. England has increased her export trade; but her home consumption has fallen away, in the matter of cotton alone, 35 per cent in three years. Value of home consumption of cotton goods, for 1866, was nearly thirteen millions; for 1868, nearly seven millions.

"In the present condition of manufacturing industries it is foolish to tell the operative class to attribute the prosperity to free trade; they are not prosperous; it is a mockery to tell them to thank God for a full stomach, when they are empty! They are *not* well off; never has starvation, pauperism, crime, discontent, been so plentiful in the manufacturing districts; never since England has been a manufacturing country has *every* industry, great or small, been so completely depressed; never has work been so impossible to find; never have the means and savings of the working classes been at so low an ebb.

"We have had periods when some two or three of the great industries were depressed, but health still remained in a number of small ones: now the depression is universal; the only industry in the country that is really flourishing is that of machine makers, turning out spinning and weaving machinery for foreign countries! many of these works are going night and day!"

Of the cotton industry, in the interests of which Great Britain threw open her ports to foreign manufactures, our author says: —

"In 1868, one-third of our total imports of raw cotton, amounting to three hundred and twenty-two and one-half million of pounds, was exported, because the merchant or importer could get more for it in the foreign markets than in our own.

"The Board of Trade returns for December, 1869, show a falling off of nearly half a million, or two and one-half per cent, in declared value of our exports, as compared with corresponding month of December, 1868 ; the falling off is chiefly in cotton goods, which are over £800,000 less than in December, 1868.

" It is not that the great cotton industry has dwindled, but that England no longer has a monopoly of it ; whilst cotton mills are closed or pulled down in England, others are being erected in considerable numbers in France, Germany, Switzerland, Belgium, and America, and the English manufacturers of cotton machinery are working early and late to execute orders for these countries. It is rather a melancholy consideration for us, but I believe it to be a fact, that the only flourishing industry in England at this moment is that of the machinists producing cotton machinery of all kinds for foreign countries."

Sir Edward refers only incidentally to the decline in the silk industry under free trade, for the reason, probably, that the facts were so well known in England that it was unnecessary to enlarge upon them ; while, on the other hand, free traders regard the facts so damaging to the cause, that they seek to suppress them. Some pertinent facts and admissions leak out in the reports and journals of commerce, which only serve to supply the omissions in the work before us. A memorial to Lord Stanley, from the working-men's association at Coventry, represents that fifty-five firms in the ribbon trade at that town have succumbed since 1860, and twelve hundred houses are vacant. In seven years before the French treaty, £8,000 were given by the parish for out-door relief; in seven years succeeding the treaty, £36,000 were given for parochial relief; for the simple reason that the importations of French ribbons, during corresponding periods, had more than quadrupled in consequence of the treaty. At a meeting of the Macclesfield Chamber of Commerce, in June, 1868, Mr. Condron said : —

" In 1826, Mr. Huskisson introduced his free-trade measures, and immediately both silk and cotton manufactures began to decline. Before the treaty came into operation, there was a great silk trade carried on in Macclesfield, and there were thousands of silk looms in Manchester ; but immediately after the commencement of the treaty, nine-tenths of the factories were closed, and machinery worth £50,000 had been sold for less than £5,000. . . . He (Mr. Condron) contended that the silk trade throughout England had been entirely annihilated by the French treaty, and the general trade of Manchester had suffered by it. The silk that should be thrown in Manchester, Macclesfield, and other places in England, was now going to France, and other foreign looms."

The Association of Chambers of Commerce suppress, as we have intimated, all reports embodying such facts as are given above.

At the annual meeting of the Association in 1869, a committee, appointed to consider foreign tariffs, presented a general report and a special report from the Chamber of Macclesfield. The question arose on the adoption of the report. The difficulty was to get rid of the Macclesfield report, which had exposed the condition of the silk industry.

" Mr. Morris, of Halifax, said the different Chambers had, of course, merely expressed their own opinions, and the meeting ought not to sanction the complaints of the operation of free trade. Any thing of that kind should be withdrawn from the report.

" Mr. Wright, of Macclesfield, said that what the manufacturers wanted, was not a system of free trade, from which some painfully suffered, but a system of fair trading between country and country; and then they would be able to compete with their foreign neighbors. . . . A manufacture was springing up in Macclesfield and elsewhere, called the mixed trade; including gentlemen's scarfs and ladies' dresses, it being partly on account of the unparalleled price of raw material. On these products France levied a duty of 10 or 20 per cent. Now, there ought to be some reciprocity in the way of duties. . . . If there was free trade *all over the world*, it would be for the benefit, not only of individuals, but of the whole community.

" Mr. Bracklehurst, M.P., remarked that Macclesfield Chamber had drawn up their report to the best of their light. The shoe had certainly pinched them very much; but whether this had arisen from the French treaty or not, he would not discuss. The trade of the town had materially diminished. Before the treaty, the importation of silk goods from France was about £750,000 value; but in 1868 it was nearly £3,000,000; and this showed how severe the competition was in that department. . . . According to the census of 1861, the silk trade employed 117,000 persons, and indirectly 300,000 were probably dependent on it. Now he was afraid the next census would show a material decrease. Pauperism was increasing enormously, and it could only be arrested by occupation being found for the people.

" Mr. Field protested emphatically, not only against several sentences in the report, but against remarks which had been made antagonistic to the principles of free trade. . . . Now he protested against the meeting being committed to doctrines of that kind. It had been suggested that such sentences should be expunged, but he thought it would be difficult to extract a *virus* which so extensively permeated the reports. It would be more prudent to accompany them with a protest against all such sentiments. He would therefore propose a rider to this effect, ' without expressing approval of any sentiments that may be found in them at variance with the doctrines of free trade.' "

To get rid of the Macclesfield report, several members recommended that none of the reports of the separate Chambers be printed. Although one member feebly protested that the facts contained in the report should go before the country, that it might " consider how to meet so serious a diminution of exports." Mr. Whitwell, M.P., pointed out that the difficulty would be met by printing none of the Chambers' reports, " as *his* report contained nothing hostile to free trade." This course was adopted by the meeting, and thus the Macclesfield report, which would have enlightened England as to the fatal influence of free trade upon one of the most important industries, was suppressed.

It is from this industry, so depressed that the free traders of England dare not publish the facts, that an American writer of Political Economy * derives an illustration of his proposition that " no branch of business grows into self-sustaining and vigorous life without the stimulating breezes of competition."

" For more than a century (he says) the silk manufacture of England, fenced round and protected, as it was called, by these restrictive and prohibitory duties, languished, pined, and at times almost expired, for the simple reason that the manufacturers, instead of relying upon their own inventive skill and energy, looked to the government for support and an artificial monopoly ; and when at length, in 1826, this

---

* Professor Perry.

foolish system was abandoned, and the silk interest was told that it must look out for itself, and the ports were thrown open to foreign silk, then first the English silk culture began to thrive. It has thriven from that day to this; until now we are told that in the plainer and firmer kinds of silk the English surpass the French, and that there is a considerable exportation of these English silks into France itself."

Sir Edward Sullivan admits that the whole English press, and the wealthy manufacturers, deny that the manufacturing interests of England are declining. We find, however, the views of Sir Edward supported by an overwhelming authority from an unexpected source.

At the annual dinner of the Chambers of Commerce of England, in March, 1868, as we find in their official reports, —

"Mr. Ripley, of Bradford, proposed the 'Textile Manufacturing Company;' with the toast, the names Mr. Bazley, M.P., Col. Akroyd, M.P., and Mr. Mundilla, as representatives of three great industries. . . . Mr. Akroyd had devoted to the interests of commerce time, talents, and money, to an extent that few had done. His establishment was held to be a model to manufacturers generally.

"Col. Akroyd, in responding in behalf of the woollen manufacturers, after a few preliminary remarks, said, 'He wished to utter a word of caution to manufacturers. Looking to the past history of the country they were apt to imagine it was impossible to lay down too much machinery, and to build too many factories. There was some limit to the products the world would take, and we are bound to admit into competition the manufacturers of Germany and France. We had other competitors in supplying the demands of the world at large, and *we could scarcely be justified in increasing our mills and machinery at the rate we had done in the past.*'"

Mildly as this singular admission is expressed by this high commercial authority, it is full of meaning. It is a declaration that the manufacturing prosperity of England has culminated under the system of free trade. With the natural increase of her population, one-fifth of which is dependent entirely upon the textile manufacture, the arresting of the increase of mills and machinery — which in former years, as from 1850 to 1859, had nearly doubled the product of the cotton manufacture in less than ten years — means inevitable decline, —a fatal decline to a nation which, in fifty years, has derived a *profit* from the manufacture of cotton alone of *one thousand millions pounds sterling.*

Under the head of "special interests," the work before us presents very lucidly the motive which induces the ruling class in England — the whole press which is its voice, and members of Parliament who are its organs — to adhere so pertinaciously to free trade. We have been led to believe that this policy is kept up, as it was established, by the great manufacturing interest. Sir Edward Sullivan shows that it is sustained by the selfish interests of the high and easy classes, the only consumers of foreign manufactures, who find great convenience and economy in the free admission of foreign manufactures in the British markets. He shows that this class oppose protection as a system of legislation for special interests; those of the operative class, because their own special interests are better secured by free trade. But, says he, —

"The special interests of some classes are, however, more urgent than those of others; for instance, the fever patient has a special interest in quinine, the *gourmet* has a special interest in truffles. But these special interests cannot be considered of equal importance; the *gourmet* can live without truffles, but the fever patient may die without quinine.

"It is the same with our own industries. The upper and middle-class consumers have a special interest in getting their luxuries cheap, as cheap as they possibly can, irrespective of the interest of the producer. The producers have a special interest in having a remunerative market for their produce; but you cannot compare the magnitude of those two interests. It is a matter of convenience and luxury to the former, of actual existence to the latter.

"In considering the effect of making England a free port, it is most important to examine and to weigh well how it affects the special interests of the different orders and classes of the community. It has been by no means general in its effect. To some classes it has been a great convenience, to others a source of great wealth, to others again a source of danger and prospective ruin.

"The admission of foreign manufactures into our markets has been a great convenience and economy to the upper and middle classes, to the rich, and to those who enjoy fixed or professional incomes, or incomes from lands. To all of them it is a decided gain; they get more for their money, their luxuries are all cheapened, and they have greater facilities for indulging in foreign tastes and fashions. The upper class, and those with fixed or professional incomes, profit by it considerably; but the class that profits by it most of all is the commercial class, — the great bankers, merchants, and brokers of the country; to them it has been the source of immense wealth. England has become a vast emporium for foreign goods and manufactures of all sorts of kinds and descriptions; English merchants are, in fact, the bankers and brokers of the goods of the whole world. Countless millions of produce and manufactures pass through their hands; and, as every item leaves some trifle behind, their business is most lucrative. An English merchant gets an order for silks, or cottons, or clocks, or watches, or the finer description of cottons and linens, for the East Indies or China, or North or South America, or Turkey, or any part of the world: it is perfectly immaterial to him whether the article he supplies has been manufactured in Manchester or Rouen, Coventry or Lyons; it does not signify the least to him whether it is British or foreign manufacture, so long as he gets his percentage.

" So long as merchants can buy foreign articles in England cheaper than British, they are quite indifferent as to the means by which this result is attained, whether by fair competition or by crafty and unjust manipulation of markets; they have nothing to do with the stoppage of mills and the ruin of manufacturers and operatives: their business is simply to buy and sell; to buy as cheap and sell as dear as they can."

It is asserted that while the operatives, the small tradesmen and householders, and the vast population that crowds the manufacturing districts, spend all their money on home-made articles, and none of it on foreign luxuries, the wealthy class, noblemen, bankers, manufacturers who increase their expenditure, spend their surplus wealth on wine, pictures, clocks, silks, satins, and articles of foreign luxury; and that, to speak roughly, nearly every manufacturing industry in England might shut up, cease to exist, and the rich and middle-class consumers, those with fixed incomes in fact, would still be supplied with every thing they require from abroad, with very little additional cost.

The author gives a remarkable illustration of the manner in which the interests of the luxurious classes are favored, in English diplomacy, in the provisions of the Anglo-French treaty.

He shows that every single one of the thirty-three or thirty-four articles, admitted duty free from France, are articles of luxury or convenience, whose use is entirely confined to the wealthier and more luxurious classes in the English community, while not a single one is directly or indirectly, or in any degree whatever, of any service to the working classes.

With such facts before the working-people, who can doubt that the masses of England will, at no brief day in the future, repudiate the calculations of the free-trade philosophy, from which their class has been excluded as a factor? As the author says, in concluding his chapter on Reciprocity, —

"The working classes have been enfranchised ; they have been urged to think and speak for themselves: and it is very probable the first use they will make of this liberty will be to protect themselves, and to tear to threads 'the puerile doctrines and illusions of their teachers, and return to the fine old national sense.'

" Even now, I believe that the most ordinary speaker, who would condescend to stump any manufacturing borough or county on the cry of ' Protection to Native Industry,' would carry it against Mr. Bright himself. Trade unions have hitherto had for their object the protection of workmen from each other, and from their employers ; soon they will seek to protect themselves and their employers against unfair foreign competition."

The writer under review regards the abolition of the corn laws as a decided legislative and social success ; but he denies, although his reasoning upon the subject is somewhat obscure, that the logical corollary of returning to protection to native industries is to return to protection of corn. The true reason why no such deduction can be made, although the author fails to state it, is that, in the then existing condition of England, the abolition of the corn laws was a measure of protection to the manufacturing class. It was a measure of *qualified protection*, a distinction first made by Mr. Bigelow ; "qualified protection," as he defines it, being "either the abrogation or adjustment of custom duties, with a view to cheapen production, and thereby aid the home producer against foreign rivalry. In the first case, raw materials are admitted free ; in the other case, duties on articles

of general consumption are increased or diminished, according
to the bearing on the cost of living, and consequently on
the rate of wages." "I freely grant," says Mr. Gladstone,
"that the relief of raw materials from taxation is a different
thing from annihilating protection." The abolition of the corn
laws was equivalent to an increase of wages to the operatives,
who threatened revolution in their clamor for relief. The bread
tax for the year 1860, with the sliding scale, and with corn at the
prices which ruled for three years before its repeal, would have
amounted to over $31,000,000. As "qualified protection" has
in view the peculiar circumstances of the nation in which it is
applied, its successful operation in England, as in the admission
of all raw materials free, is no argument for its adoption in a nation placed in altogether different circumstances. For instance,
England admitted wool free of duty. This was a boon to manufacturers, but no injury to agriculture. England raises only
mutton sheep. Her climate prevents the culture of merinos.
With the command of the best long-woolled sheep in the world,
she had no fear of competition with her wool from foreign nations.
Her lands were already occupied by all the flocks which they
could nourish. The production of wool could not, therefore, be
stimulated by any duty. Besides, sheep are grown in England
primarily for mutton, the wool being only the incident. Animals,
unlike wool, are, in an insular country, almost completely protected by expense of transportation. The repeal of the corn laws,
and the enlarged purchasing power of one-fifth of the whole population dependent on manufactures, increasing the consumption of
animal food, made the improved market for mutton an ample com-
pensation for the repeal of the duty on wool. It is needless to
observe that the conditions of sheep husbandry in this country find
no parallel with those enumerated as peculiar to England. To
demand, upon the authority of English example, the repeal of the
wool duties here, which are essential to keep up the supply of
four-fifths of the consumption of our mills, is as unreasonable as
it is preposterous to hope to accomplish it while the agricultural
class, being the most numerous, have a just claim for the regard
to their rights and interests, and also have the political power
to enforce them.

We have already remarked that it is the object of Sir Edward Sullivan less to prove his case by an array of facts and statistics than to utter his earnest convictions.

The fundamental truths upon which his argument reposes — viz., that the former advance of England in manufacturing prosperity was in spite of free trade, and that the present decline is due to it — require but very simple statements or illustrations. Still, we may gather some incidental facts which are instructive, and which we present without any attempt at systematic arrangement, leaving to the reader to apply them.

The facts given as the operation of the Anglo-French treaty are peculiarly interesting, in view of the reference which is so often made to this treaty as an illustration of the progress of free economical philosophy. An American writer upon political economy,* speaking of this treaty, observes : " A large part of the manufactures of either country are admitted into the other with perfect freedom, and the duties on most of the rest very materially reduced ; and the French manufacturers have found, as the American at no distant day will find, that there is nothing which stimulates manufactures so much as a broad market, — not merely a home market, but a world market. The French sent to England, in 1863, 1,176,000,000 francs' worth of goods, and received back within a trifle as much in return, which was almost a quarter of what they sent and received to and from the rest of the world."

Upon consulting the French treaty and the pages of Sir Edward Sullivan, we find a very different story. France admitted free not a single article of textile manufactures except thrown silk, which was wanted as a raw material, and a few articles of miscellaneous manufacture, such as tiles, bricks, and gas retorts, also wanted to supply her manufacturers, and artificial flowers and modes, which was admitting coals to Newcastle ; but she did admit brandies, silk, glass, mirrors, china, carriages, cabinet-ware, and thirty or more other articles which are actually produced more cheaply in France than in England, at an *ad valorem* duty

---

* Professor Perry.

4

of 15 per cent. In 1865, according to our author, the total exports from England to France amounted to twenty-five and one-half millions sterling. The exports from France to England amounted to fifty-three millions, of which over forty millions were French products and manufactures. Our author continues : —

" The relative value of this international trade is shown more by its nature than by its amount. It was nearly as follows : *seventy-two per cent* of our exports to France were raw materials (seven-eighths of which were foreign and colonial produce, merely passing through the country, and one-eighth coal and iron). *Sixteen per cent* were half raw materials, chiefly yarns of different descriptions, on which most of the labor remained to be done in France. *Twelve per cent* only were fully manufactured articles ; a very large proportion of which consisted in the machinery of all kinds required to manufacture the raw and half raw materials we supplied them with.

" Our manufactured goods paid duties from 27½ per cent on glass and potteries, to 20 per cent on cutlery, 13 per cent on cotton, to 7½ on metal work.

" Of our imports from France, 16 per cent were raw materials ; all home produce, consisting chiefly of brandy, wines, oil, corn, &c., true produce of the soil, annual and inexhaustible, and on which a vast amount of labor had been employed.

" *Thirty-one per cent* were half raw materials, and 52½ per cent were fully manufactured articles, on which all the labor was employed in France, and all of which were admitted duty free in England.

" It is thus a fact, that 88 per cent of the articles exported from England to France, in 1865, consisted of foreign and colonial raw produce, on which no labor had been expended in this country, and of half raw materials, on which comparatively little had been employed, and of the coal and iron necessary to manufacture them ; whilst of the remaining 12 per cent, a very considerable proportion consisted of spinning and weaving, and other machinery necessary to extend the manufacturing industries of the country.

" This was in 1865. Take a later date. In the debate in the French Chambers, Jan. 18, 1870, Monsieur Johnstone said : ' Our exports to England are four times as large as our importations from that country ; we have exported goods to the value of four hundred millions of francs more than we have imported.' And still, in the face of statements and facts such as these, we find free-trade orators and free-trade penny-a-liners calling on the producing class to be thankful for the blessings they derive from free trade.

"According to this statement of the exchange of the manufactured products of the two countries in 1865, the French exported to us , seven times the value of manufactured goods we exported to them; to do this, they must have expended seven times as much in wages, and found occupation for seven times as many hands."

The wilful misrepresentations in respect to this treaty, made to the people by free-trade advocates, is thus exposed : —

"Public men have stated, in addressing the working classes, that our exports of cotton to France alone exceeded thirteen millions per annum; and they have asked them what they would have done but for this market for such a large portion of their produce. But they knew perfectly well that nine-tenths of this cotton exported to France was either in the raw state, merely passing through the country, or cotton in a half manufactured state. Misrepresentations of the comparative competing powers of ourselves and foreigners are cruel deceits to practise on the ignorance of the operative class, and they have a perfect right to, and in all probability will some day, resent them."

The figures as to the balance of trade, in which the author says he is not ashamed to believe, considering it a matter of very serious import that every year the balance of trade against England should increase, are thus stated : —

"In 1854 the balance against us was			. . . .	37	millions.
1855	,,	,,	,,	. . . .	27	,,
1856	,,	,,	,,	. . . .	33	,,
1857	,,	,,	,,	. . . .	41	,,
1858	,,	,,	,,	. . . .	25	,,
1859	,,	,,	,,	. . . .	14	,,
1860	,,	,,	,,	. . . .	45	,,
1861	,,	,,	,,	. . . .	58	,,
1862	,,	,,	,,	. . . .	59	,,
1863	,,	,,	,,	. . . .	52	,,
1864	,,	,,	,,	. . . .	62	,,
1865	,,	,,	,,	. . . .	53	,,
1866	,,	,,	,,	. . . .	57	,,
1867	,,	,,	,,	. . . .	50	,,
1868	,,	,,	,,	. . . .	68	,,

" In 1869, it is stated, it will be over one hundred millions. In 1854, our imports exceeded our exports by thirty-seven millions; in 1847, by forty-one millions; in 1868, by sixty-eight millions; so that, in fourteen years, the annual balance against us, in our export and import trade, has advanced from thirty-seven to sixty-eight millions, and the total against us amounts to nearly seven hundred millions. Remember, this is a quantitative comparison; the meaning of it is, that, in 1868, we buy more and sell less, in comparison to our whole trade, to the extent of thirty-one millions, than we did in 1854.

" As I have before remarked, the fact that, during the last twelve or fourteen years, the excess of imports over exports amounts to over seven hundred millions sterling, is a proof of the immense wealth of the country, but no proof at all that the wealth is increasing; on the contrary, the accumulated wealth of the country must have diminished."

While the author maintains that the tide of wealth now ebbing from England would flow back, if free trade were adopted by the other principal nations, he has no hope of such a consummation. He says : —

" Protection is as firmly drawn around all the native industries of Europe and America as it was twenty years ago, and generations will elapse before there is any sensible move in the opposite direction. If the English operative class are to wait till universal free trade overspreads the world, England must be turned into a Sleepy Hollow, to be awakened every hundred years, to see how foreigners are learning their duty to their neighbors as well as to themselves.

" We are told free-trade principles are spreading; why, in Prussia, Austria, Belgium, Switzerland, the idea even of opening their ports and markets, and inviting competition with their own industrial population, has never yet been mooted : whilst in America, the operative's paradise, the duties on many British manufactures have been doubled during the last few years; and France, the Promised Land of free trade, is already trying to withdraw the nominal facilities doled out to us in the commercial treaty. The only man in France who is at heart a free trader, is the emperor himself."

The reactionists in England against free trade, as it exists there, do not yet acknowledge themselves to be protectionists. They limit themselves to demanding reciprocity. They say : " Give us reciprocity. Get other nations to take all their duties off, and we shall be content; let us close our ports to nations who will not reciprocate, and we shall have real free trade in one." Such a party has already rallied in Coventry, and resolutions in favor of reciprocity were passed at a public meeting. By whatever name the reactionary party is called, it no less represents protective sentiments. Several pamphlets which have recently appeared, give earnest utterance to the extensive dissatisfaction prevailing among the manufacturers, in relation to the working of the free-trade policy. One before us, printed in 1869, is entitled "The Present and Long-continued Stagnation of Trade; its Causes, Effects, and Cure: by a Manchester Man." The writer is Mr. R. Burn. Another tract is entitled "Free Trade, a Gigantic Mistake: by James Roberts." As the arguments and facts are of the same tenor as those already given in the lengthy quotations from Sir Edward Sullivan, we shall content ourselves with a single extract from each pamphlet, bearing upon the fundamental fact, the decline of manufacturing prosperity in England. Mr. Burn, of Manchester, says:—

"The trade of this country has fallen into such a deplorable position, that there is scarcely a single branch of it which does not leave a very heavy loss to the producers, and consequently little inducement for the investment of capital and the employment of labor; indeed, the amount of distress that at present pervades the industrial interests of this kingdom is truly deplorable, and the future appears still more clouded than the present.

"The cause of such a state of things, I feel very sure, arises almost exclusively from foreign competition, which has increased to such an extent that, a few years since, would have been thought fabulous, and no doubt was not anticipated by the most acute politicians a quarter of a century ago. It was then thought, that as manufacturers we reigned supreme, and could defy all competition. However, experience has proved the reverse; and we now find that, unless we can obtain foreign reciprocity, even by begging that which we could once have commanded, we must descend to a position lower than that which we at present hold."

Mr. Roberts states thus in detail the industries which are suffering:—

"In order to explain and account for the injuries to British manufacturing trades, it is necessary that we should show how foreign competition, and the admission of foreign manufactures duty free, are affecting the British workman ; and we will now cite cases, by way of illustration, which have come under our notice in a variety of ways, and are very varied in their character.

" We find that Millwall, Deptford, Woolwich, and most ship-building ports, are comparatively idle ; no sailing vessels building : foreign vessels do away with the necessity for British. Trade falls off in the towns of Nottingham, Macclesfield, Stockport, Bolton, Wigan, Oldham, Coventry, Leek, Preston, Manchester, Derby, Congleton, Sandbach, Leighton, Buzzard, Luton, Newport, Pagnell, Tring, Exeter, Crediton, and London, and many other places. Ship-building involves thirty other trades ; watch-making, sixty trades : they are gradually passing from us. The iron trade is losing ground ; tools, chairs, pans, spades, hoes, axes, nails, lamps, tin-ware, locks, curry-combs, traps, hinges, brass foundry, needles, hooks, guns, swords, buttons, jewelry, steel pens, trinkets, pins, wire, tubing, scales, cutlery, bronze articles, japanned articles, &c., &c., now come from America, France, and Germany. We have doors, window-sashes, and all kinds of woodwork, from the Baltic. Foreign agricultural implements, furniture, artificial flowers, baby-linen, dresses, baskets, beads, beds, Berlin work, blankets, bonnets, boots, braids, brushes, candles, canes, common carpets, cardboards, caps, china, glass of every kind, clocks, cloths, damasks, delaine, electrotype paper, pencils, fringe, muslin, lace, gilded goods, gold and silver articles, hosiery, leather, linen, looking-glasses, lucifers, shoes, silk, ribbons, soap, stationery, stays, steam-engines,— in fact every thing, small and great ; and all are admitted duty free into England, and on equal terms into our colonies.

" Is it, then, any matter of surprise that the British workmen and British manufacturers have no employment ? If all these articles were made here, there would be no lack of work for the British workman ; and the whole of England would once more be set in motion."

M. Emile de Laveleye, an eminent French political economist, but not of the protective school, has recently furnished to the "Revue des Deux Mondes" a very instructive article upon the "land question" in England. After showing that the accumulation of capital in the little island of Great Britain is so vast, that the vaunted treasures of Carthage, Tyre, and Babylon are nothing by its side, he adduces many facts which confirm the statements of the English authorities already quoted, as to the present

unparalleled distress of the working classes in England. He
shows that pauperism, which had before slightly diminished, had
increased since 1866. The number of persons relieved, which
in January, 1866, was 920,344, rose in January, 1869, to
1,039,549, in a total population of 21,760,000 ; that is, in England, exclusive of Scotland and Ireland. Although in the last
year 167,000 emigrants had left room for those who remained,
the number of paupers had increased in that year 74,000. He
quotes the observation of Lord Hamilton in Parliament, that
"it is impossible to consult the sad statements which indicate a
constant increase of misery for the three years past, without being vividly alarmed for the future." M. Laveleye remarks that
this increase of wealth on the one hand, and of misery on the
other, overturns all the old calculations of the science of political
economy. "The economists say that if a considerable part of
mankind is still poorly provided with the necessaries of life, it is
because labor does not produce enough. This would seem true.
Then the genius of invention accomplishes wonders. It constructs
machines so admirable, that a single individual can do the work
which once required a thousand. According to Mr. Fairbairn,
an English engineer, the total number of horse-powers employed
on the steam engines of England, in 1865, was 3,650,000, equivalent to the labor of seventy-six millions workmen. There are
in that country about five millions families. Each family, then,
has at its service fifteen slaves, whose muscles of steel, put in
motion by coal, are never tired. Among those peoples who have
not yet learned how to borrow from nature these indefatigable
servants, — in Russia, for example, — the labor of the head
of a family, using the most simple tools, is sufficient to provide
comfortably for all his dependants. How is it that every Eng-
lishman, having at his command fifteen slaves, is not able to live
in the greatest comfort? M. F. Passy, in his work on Machines,
repeats a calculation which proves that England, in 1860, exported 2,673,960 kilograms in weight of cotton cloth, or sixty-
four times the circumference of the earth. How is it that she
can send abroad the vestment for our planet, when she cannot
clothe her own poor?"

The writer seeks, with English economists, — Mill, Leslie, Fawcett, and Bright, — to explain the exceptional situation in which England finds herself, by the land monopoly, which excludes the whole working population from any interest in the soil. Potential as this cause unquestionably is, M. Laveleye almost unconsciously admits, in the following passage, the influence of a more efficient cause ; viz., unrestricted foreign competition with English industry. Comparing the present condition of industry with that under the old *régime*, he says : " Now, on the contrary, in the economic world all is agitation, uncertainty, strife, incessant alternatives of progress and crises. This is the result of the division of labor, which makes all the industries dependent on each other ; of the employment of mechanical forces, which group an increasing number of workmen, with increasing wages, in the same establishment ; and of the facility of international exchanges, which places each one in competition with unknown rivals scattered throughout the whole world. The great industry does not work for the clientage of the neighborhood which it can understand, but for the market of the world, whose necessities it is impossible to foresee. The dearness of food or raw material, a revolution, a war, a change of tastes, a crowd of other circumstances, may close the outlets of production, and bring on ruin. The workmen share the chances of their employers ; a new engine, a displaced industry, may force them to change their occupation or residence. No one, neither patron nor workman, is sure of the morrow. Such is the situation which we see everywhere around us. It gives rise to the complaints which we hear from time to time, on the part of masters as well as workmen ; but without re-establishing the *régime* of the Middle Ages, or finding a wholly new organization, whose elements we cannot yet resolve, it is difficult to escape from a situation which is the result of economic liberty, free competition (*la concurrence*), and the condition of industrial progress. To this general uncertainty of conditions, we must now add another source of complaints and troubles. It is the strife between labor and capital. It is a general hostility, a veritable social war, of which the arms of combat are coalitions and strikes. It is not for political rights that they are undertaken; it is, what is much more agonizing, for the means of existence. It is the ' struggle for life,' of which naturalists speak, transported from the animal world to the economical world. The manufacturing employer, pushed by free competition, is obliged to demand the utmost possible work for the least possible wages. The workman, on his side, is driven to obtain the most wages from the least work. The conflict, far from subsiding, becomes more general, and nowhere has taken more alarming proportions than in England." What can be more graphic than this sketch of the results of free trade, drawn by one who is compelled, by theory, to accept a system whose lamentable consequences he deplores !

It is the vaunted economic liberty, the unrestrained competition from abroad, the contempt for home demand, the ambition to supply the world, the system of production at the cheapest possible rate for the utmost possible production, which have cast the people of England into the " struggle for life," upon which the upper classes look down, from the amphitheatre of exalted position, as the Romans looked upon the struggles of the arena. We have to thank M. Laveleye for the illustration which he has drawn from the animal world, and we will venture to complete it.

Mr. Darwin, to whom we owe the phrase above quoted, and the first elucidation of a great principle of nature which it expresses, has shown that, in the free strife for existence to which nature has left the feral races of the animal world, it is the *strongest*, and not the *best* merely, which have swept race after race from the earth ; for many of the extinct forms are grander than those which survive. He shows, too, that it is through an unrestricted range over the continents, unprotected by barriers of mountain ranges or intervening oceans, that the domain of the surviving races has been extended. The barriers of mountains, oceans, rivers, and climates, have alone preserved the characteristic features of those regions which retain their peculiar types of animal or vegetable existence. These natural obstructions have given variety to the productions of the earth, and break up that drear monotony which would have followed from the unimpeded sway of the strongest races.

5

So it is in the industrial world. In the economical competition of nations, it is not the best and fittest industries which
survive; it is those of the strongest people. Unobstructed in
their admission to India and Turkey, British cottons have sup-
planted the magnificent muslins of Hindostan; and the cheap
dress goods of Bradford have extinguished the precious mohair
fabrics of Angora, just as the white-weed and Canada thistle
take possession of the blue-grass pastures of the West. They
supplant, but they by no means replace. Protective barriers
are to industrial nations what natural obstructions are to the
animal and vegetable world. They secure to each country its
native industries, and permit others to take root, which, in time,
acquire a national character, impressed by the peculiar genius of
each people. The arts and products of each country overflow
its borders, and spread into surrounding nations. The whole
world is benefited by the variety, excellence, and cheapness,
which follow from the competition of many industrial countries,
deriving their very power to compete from partial exemption
from competition; and is relieved from the monotony, medi-
ocrity, and dearness of production, which are the inevitable
results of a monopoly of industries by the strongest and wealth-
iest nation.

LOUIS ADOLPHE THIERS AND FRANCE.

Amidst the crash which announces to us, as we write, the fall
of the proudest nation of Europe, and the displacement of the
political axis of a continent, it seems almost mistimed to turn
to France for any other lessons than the vanity of human ambition, and the instability of a national glory which has no other
defence than imperial will. As a military nation, France is, to
all appearance, annihilated. But she lives, and will continue
to live, in her science and art, in her taste which rules the empire of fashion; and, above all, in the supremacy of her industry,
which the genius of her workmen and the perfection of their
productions have made the *best*, if not the most powerful, among
all the industries of modern nations. The example and lessons
of such a country will be still studied by all nations who desire to

attain material prosperity. The country which, in Colbert, gave to the world the great apostle of the protective philosophy, has in the most cherished of her living historians and statesmen the best expounder of his doctrines. We propose, in further illustration of our general theme, "The Protective Sentiment Abroad," to present the substance of a recent discourse by this eminent man, after submitting some brief biographical notes, to enforce the weight of authority with which he speaks upon economical questions.

Louis Adolphe Thiers was born at Marseilles, in France, April 16th, 1797. The son of a poor workman, an origin in which he has always gloried, he was, through the patronage of influential maternal relations, enabled to receive a classical education. After distinguishing himself at college, he studied law, and, entering upon his profession, made some efforts which gave promise of a brilliant career. He was, however, early led away by the higher attractions of history and philosophy. Completing ten volumes of the " History of the French Revolution," a work commenced by another author, he at once attained celebrity as a historian. He became equally well known as a shrewd political writer and literary critic, through his contributions to the journals, and a volume on the fine arts, and one of travels. In 1830 he established, with Mignet and Armand Carrel, a new political journal, the "National," which, more than any other, contributed to bring about the Revolution of that year.

After rising to distinction in the Chamber of Deputies, to which he had been elected through the political influence acquired as a journalist, he became, in 1832, Minister of the Interior, and shortly afterwards Minister of Commerce. His administration was signalized by the new impulse given to internal improvements, and the fostering care afforded to industry. In 1836 he rose to the Premiership of France. Being unable to persuade the King, Louis Philippe, to adopt a more liberal policy at home and more energy in his transactions abroad, he resigned, but was reinstated in 1840. While Premier, he set himself at work, with extraordinary vigor, to prepare the country for war; which he deemed necessary to raise France to her

proper standing, outwitted as she had been by the diplomacy of
Russia, Austria, and England, in respect to the Eastern question. He prepared for this emergency, by reinforcing the
regular army, reorganizing the National Guards; and by con-
structing the fortifications of Paris, which he has lived to see
the last refuge of the Capital. Unable, however, to make the
King partake of his war views, he resigned the Premiership,
and has not again been called to the administrative control of
public affairs.

From 1845 to 1848 he figured as one of the opposition
leaders to the Guizot cabinet, and was prominent in denoun-
cing the growing influence of the Jesuits. His speeches were
eagerly read and commented upon; and his articles in the
"Constitutionel," in the ownership of which he had a share,
contributed to the spread of the reform agitation. In 1846 he
denounced the cabinet for declaring itself against the annexation
of Texas to the United States, under the poor pretence of
preserving an *American equilibrium,* which was in reality only
an English equilibrium; and thus, as he expressed it, "alien-
ating France from the great American nation, which is destined
to effect the enfranchisement of our political system."

Although M. Thiers voted for the Presidency of Louis
Napoleon, he pronounced, only fifteen days before the *coup
d'état,* while demanding the independence of the Assembly, as
it were the funeral oration of the Republic, by predicting that
it was perhaps the last Assembly which should really represent
France. The political seer, who had penetrated the designs of
the imperial usurper, could not fail to fall under his ban. Thiers
was imprisoned, and afterwards temporarily banished. He was
shortly after permitted to return, when he abandoned politics,
and entered upon the completion of his great work, the "History of the Consulate and the Empire," — a work published in
20 volumes, which has been translated into every language in
Europe; and, in 1863, won for its author, from the Institute
of France, the extraordinary prize of 20,000 francs. As we
have more to do with M. Thiers as a practical statesman than
as a historian, we will pass by this work, with the single quo-

tation of its concluding sentence, — a passage which reveals the liberal, and at the same time conservative, tone which characterizes the political opinions of a statesman writing history which he has helped to make : —

" The life of this great man, so instructive for soldiers, rulers, and politicians, contains a lesson also to citizens. It teaches them that they ought never to abandon their country to the power of one man, no matter who he may be, no matter under what circumstances ! This is the cry which springs from my heart, the sincere wish I utter as I conclude this long history of our triumphs and our successes, and which I hope will penetrate the heart of every Frenchman, and persuade him never to sacrifice his liberty, nor run the risk of doing so, by abusing it."

In 1863, M. Thiers reappeared upon the political stage as a member of the *Corps Législatif*, being one of nine deputies, of liberal politics, returned by the city of Paris. He at once took the first place in the opposition, as the defender of the public liberties ; and his discourses, always carefully prepared for the press, were eagerly read by the country, if not religiously listened to by the Assembly. In the recent events M. Thiers has been conspicuous for the sagacity with which he pronounced upon the want of preparation, on the part of France, for the terrible struggle into which the Emperor had so rashly rushed ; and for the patriotic forbearance which withheld him from discouraging the army by an expression of his views. The Assembly evinced its confidence in his wisdom and vast military sagacity, by electing him, against his own remonstrance, without a dissenting voice, a member of the Committee of Defence. His own country, as well as Europe, has listened to every word which has fallen from his lips, with an eagerness which has sufficiently recognized him as the first of the statesmen of France.

It is said by his biographers, in pronouncing upon his forensic powers, that it is not the style of his discourses, — though declared at times to have attained the most austere beauties of eloquence, — nor his stature or voice, which make M. Thiers a great orator, but it is " the intelligence and good sense

which he exhibits in an incomparable degree." Of his character as a statesman, it is said, "that among the men who
served Louis Philippe, that which distinguished M. Thiers
in a remarkable degree is his vivid sentiment of national
dignity, and a sort of practical genius, which enabled him
to govern otherwise than by pure formulas of political theory.
Enamoured with the wonders of art and the grandeurs of industry, he has always applied his thoughts to the first necessities
of a nation." Again it is said : "One of the most remarkable
characteristics of the talent of M. Thiers is a powerful faculty of
assimilation in the presence of things the most unlike, the relations of which he is able to seize at once, and which he is able
to unite into a system full of lucidity and practical utility. The
different consulative committees of commerce, manufactures, and
agriculture, which he frequently called together, under his presidency as Minister of Public Works, and whose apparently opposite interests he sought to reconcile, brought out particularly
this eminent quality."

If the views of a statesman so eminently practical, upon the
most practical of all public questions, outweigh all the theories
of schoolmen and closet essayists, the passages which follow,
and which we have translated from "L'Opinion Nationale," are
the truest expression of the protective sentiment of France.

The question of an inquiry into the operation of the commercial treaties being before the *Corps Législatif*, M. Thiers, on the
22d of January, 1870, after calling attention to the gravity of
the question before the Assembly, addressed it as follows : —

" Every nation has three great affairs, which should be the object of
its ardent and constant solicitude : liberty first, its greatness next,
and finally its material prosperity.   Liberty, which consists not merely
in the right of the nation to criticise its government, but in the right
of governing itself by its own hands, and conformably to its own
ideas ; greatness, which does not consist in subjecting its neighbors
by brute force, but in exercising over them so much influence
that no question shall be resolved in the world against its interests
and security ; prosperity, finally, which consists in drawing from its

own soil, and from the genius of its inhabitants, the greatest possible amount of well-being.

" And do not think that this anxiety for the prosperity of the country has any thing in common with that passion for material interests which the highest minds despise. There is no work of higher morality than to diminish the sum of the evils which weigh upon man, even in the most civilized societies. To make man less unhappy, — that is, to make him better, — it is to make him more just towards his government, to his fellow-beings, towards Providence itself.

" We have before us a noble task : we shall succeed, I hope, in accomplishing it. It is to give to the country liberty, without disturbance, without violence, without revolution. The work of establishing prosperity where it is wanting is not less grand or less worthy of your thoughts.

" The Government has thought, for a time, that it could arrogate, for itself alone, the right of deciding upon the economical system of the country. I do not wish to recriminate as to the past : this is not the time. We must, on the contrary, forget the past, or remember the past only to derive from it instruction. Our task is to fecundate the present and the future.

" It was nevertheless a strange pretension, that of thinking that the Government could, of itself alone, decide upon the economical system of the country. I can understand that the Government — when it is composed of the most enlightened men of the country — might believe that it could be a better diplomat, a better warrior, than the mass of the nation; but a better merchant, a better manufacturer, a better agriculturist, when the nation is composed of merchants, manufacturers, and agriculturists, is an unsustainable pretension."

After appealing to the Assembly to listen to details, however dry, without which they would have in mind only vague generalities, without practical utility, M. Thiers continues : —

" I have exhausted myself in this study, to which I have brought the greatest material disinterestedness, and that moral disinterestedness, which results from the absence of bias for any system. I shall proceed directly to the end which we have in view. In these debates some call themselves protectionists, others free traders, and we have even heard the term compensationists. I accept whatever term you will. It is the *thing* only which I have in view.

" It is asked, Shall we place around France a sort of Chinese wall ?

No : our object is the national labor, which we wish to preserve in the
country ; to give birth to it where it does not exist ; but, above all,
to preserve it where it does exist. Do we demand, for this, prohibitive
duties ? . No. Duties sufficiently protective ? Not even that."

After briefly showing that the duties in France are not sufficient to preserve such national industry as is already established,
he resumes : —

" I can understand that we might hesitate before undertaking to develop certain industries in a country ; but what I cannot understand is,
that, when they are already developed, we should leave them to perish.
" We are told that we would have a hot-house industry. What, then,
are the nations which have sought to develop among themselves a national labor ? They are the nations which are intelligent and free. When
the foreigner brings them a product, after they have found it serviec-
able, they desire to imitate it. The nations which do not have this
desire are the indolent nations of the East ; intelligent and free nations
seek to appropriate for themselves the products brought to them by
foreign nations.
" We are constantly referred to England. Here is an example
which this great and intelligent nation has given us. In the four-
teenth, fifteenth, and sixteenth centuries, the people of the Low countries had become enriched by the beautiful products of their woollen
manufactures ; England, who had received these products, as soon as
she commenced to wake up to her position, said to herself, ' It is out of
my wools that these tissues are fabricated. I have the hands, the intelligence, the raw material ; and shall the labor of foreigners provide
me with my necessities ? ' She kept her wools : she put herself to
work ; and then commenced the great prosperity of England. Was
there any barbarism in that ? I am asked, Did not England soon
after renounce this system ? I answer by the question, Did not
England, only a few years ago, in order to procure for herself the
beautiful industry of flax and linens, cover herself with protective
tariffs, forbid the exportation of machines, and even give premiums to
the peasants of Ireland to encourage the production of flax ?
" I wish it were in my power to conduct you through the history of
civilization. I could show you that there has been no intelligent nation, which has not held it, not only for its profit, but for its honor, to
create for itself the productions of other nations, whenever nature
did not oppose it.

" I need not recall Colbert, creating our marine, our woollen industry, our silk industry, our lace manufactures, our glass industry, and for this purpose giving, according to the language of the times, the money of the king, the lands of the king, and even nobility itself, which was at the king's disposal.

"This is old-time history, you say. I will lead you to the youngest and freest nations. You shall see that the procedures of two centuries ago are still their procedures. An English member of Parliament, Sir Wentworth Dilke, who has travelled over all the English possessions, has recently published a remarkable book, in which you will find a curious picture of the vast Britannic Empire. I would have those who think themselves at the head of the science of political economy, and who scoff at the protective system, read this book. They would see that it is not America alone which covers herself with protective tariffs to develop her own labor : the English Colonies, Canada, and Australia, have recourse to the most energetic tariffs against their own metropolis, to establish industries upon their own soil. India herself, which has a colony of 500,000 English established upon her territory, makes tariffs, that its cotton may be manufactured by herself. And Sir Wentworth Dilke repeats the words spiritedly uttered by America of the West : ' An agricultural people should become a manufacturing people. We want something besides the seaboard capitals, New York and Boston. We want to sustain the brilliant cities of the interior, such as Cincinnati and Chicago ; and to do this, we must exclude, by means of protection, the productions of foreign nations.'

" And nevertheless Sir Wentworth Dilke is a free trader in England ; but he comprehends that what suits one country does not suit all, and that *free trade is not the law of the world.*

" But I lay aside theory, to return to it again, and proceed to the facts which touch us so nearly."

M. Thiers then proceeds to point out the circumstances which characterize the state of the leading industries of France, under the operation of the treaties of Commerce, with the free-trade tendency impressed upon them by the arbitrary act of the government which concluded them. The order which he proposes in this discussion is instructive : —

" Since all the industries have man for their object and instrument, I shall take as my guiding thread in this debate the order of the neces-

sities of man. It is necessary that man should clothe himself ; that he
should procure for himself a covering ; that he should feed himself; and,
finally, put himself in communication with the world. I shall examine these according to their logical order, — the textile industries,
those of construction and iron, agriculture, and the merchant marine."

It would be beyond our purpose to follow the orator in details
which have special relation to the interests of France : we shall
limit ourselves to extracts which are instructive to our own industry, or throw light upon the general question of protection.

It is sometimes said that the American cotton manufacture can
contend, without the aid of tariffs, against the cotton manufacture of Great Britain.   Let those who assert this be instructed
by what M. Thiers says of the incapacity of France for such a
contest : —

"Cotton is the grand textile of modern times. It was not unknown
to the ancients. Egypt shows us cotton stuffs dating four or five thousand years ago. What is the importance of the industry of cotton
among us ? We work up 600,000 or 700,000 bales, which represent in
weight 90,000,000 of kilograms, and in value 300,000,000 of francs.
When the cotton has been spun, woven, converted into plain cloths,
printed cloths, haberdashery, and hoisery, these 300,000,000 of francs
represent 11,000,000 or 12,000,000 of francs. No industry has superior or equal importance. What is its peril ? It is exposed to a double
rivalry, that of the English and of the Swiss.
"The English find the material, in part upon their own possessions
and part abroad. They have created among themselves an immense
market, and it is not possible that we can seriously speak of making
Havre the equivalent of England. The English have over us immense advantages : great capital, raw material, an enormous commerce, machines in the greatest number, coal at the cheapest price,
and finally, which is a capital point, have the cheapness which results
from an immense production. Whilst we move 6,000,000 of spindles,
they move 34,000,000 ; we work up 600,000 or 700,000 bales of cotton,
they work up 3,000,000. Hence the cheapness which creates the grand
production by lowering the general expenses. . . . It is very difficult to
establish the true prices of production, I know : but, for myself, I am
sure that the difference in the cost of production between England and
France is not less than 15 or 20 per cent."

The advantage of the Swiss cotton manufacturers over the French is estimated by M. Thiers at 25 per cent.

After reviewing the state of the flax manufacture, and coming to the woollen industry, M. Thiers regards the industry of merinos, like that of silks, so dominant that it fears no competitor. The mixed stuffs of wool and cotton, he says, are with difficulty sustained in competition with those of England. The fine clothing industry has nothing to fear; but with the inferior stuffs, made of waste material, the English, says M. Thiers, overwhelm France. " The most hideous and tainted rags are disinfected, carded, transformed into a kind of oakum, then into yarn without solidity, and made into tissues, which, instead of 10 or 12 francs, costs 4 francs the yard. Whilst we formerly made for the people excellent cloths, entirely of wool, and which could not be worn out, we give them at present these detestable stuffs ; and this for the profit of foreigners." We need not say that our wool and woollen tariff has delivered the United States from an inundation of these "detestable stuffs," of which the English blankets, costing 18 or 20 cents per lb., are a type, and whose exclusion, by a duty of 200 or 300 per cent, is the gravest charge which the free traders can make against our tariff.

Proceeding to a discussion of the existing state of agriculture in France, M. Thiers calls attention to the hundreds of letters which he has received, complaining of its decline, especially in the wool-growing districts, and to a petition signed by more than a thousand agriculturists of Campiègne, who say that the price of wools has decreased 40 per cent, and that mutton is sold with difficulty since it meets in the markets of Paris the English and German competition.

He asks, Is it true that wools which we have seen at 1 franc 50 centimes bring now only 71 centimes? A voice in the Chambers answers that it is unquestionable. M. Thiers proceeds : —

" In certain countries where they have pasturage analogous to that of England, and the culture of the large-sized animals has succeeded, the culture of the English sheep, which produce much mutton and wool, has also succeeded ; but upon four-fifths of the territory, where the soil is stony, and only the fine grasses abound, the fine sheep alone

can convert this grass into flesh and manure. But it is threatened
that this French sheep must disappear from the soil. (Cries from the
Chamber, ' It is true.') The wools of Australia do not possess all the
qualities of the French wool. They are not so silky, so fine, so supple,
and, above all, so tenacious ; but they are very excellent, and they are
able to make a very formidable competition, because the pastures in
Australia are immense, the internal duties are small, and because
the facility of transportation permits these wools to be landed upon
our shores at very low prices.

"Our ovine population has gone down from 40,000,000 to 30,000,-
000. Our production of wool is 65,000,000 kilograms, and we
import 90,000,000. Australia already gives 165,000,000, and she
will give 300,000,000 if they are wanted. La Plata can produce
as much more.

" In this situation how can the French resist the foreign competition ?
The agricultural industry of France cannot dispense with sheep. The
facts which I have given ought to inspire you with the most serious
concern."

In the replication which M. Thiers made to the arguments
of the free traders, on the 26th of January, he refers again to
the question of wools : —

" A young and very intelligent traveller, M. de Beaumont, has given
some curious details about Australia. The wool-growers who commenced with 150,000 francs make as much as 500,000 francs in a
year. The reason is that the land costs nothing ; there are no taxes ;
and a man on horseback can take care of 1000 sheep. Australia will
soon export 200,000,000 or 300,000,000 of kilograms. La Plata
and the Cape of Good Hope will soon reach the same number.

" I do not wish to prevent your resorting to these countries. Protection as well as free trade follows the progress of science. But with an
indigenous production of 65,000,000 of kilograms, in presence of a
foreign exportation which may reach 600,000,000, can you be tranquil?

" We are told, Make mutton. Have you ever seen sheep producing
mutton and no wool ? You say to agriculture, Grow sheep which
produce the most mutton and the most wool. This unhappy agriculture, which you accuse of being all routine, has tried the English
sheep in the north of France. It does not think much of it. Is the
essay practicable everywhere ? Ask our agriculturists ? They
will tell you that in the centre, the east, the south, the rustic sheep,

the old French sheep, is the only one possible. There are no districts having pastures which will grow the mutton sheep, and for four-fifths of the territory the production of 65,000,000 of kilograms remains, in the face of a foreign production which can reach up to 600,000,000 of kilograms.

" If this situation does not impress you, it is because you are optimists ; and this no one has a right to be except for his own affairs. When it concerns the fortune of the community, optimism is nothing but blind improvidence."

We have reproduced these passages at length, because we regard them as worthy of profound attention. They completely disprove the statement of the late special Commissioner of the Revenue, already denied by the Executive Committee of our Wool Manufacturers' Association, that the experience in France has been " high duty, low wool at home ; moderate duty or free wool, prices good at home." They establish the important proposition that *the agriculture of a nation cannot dispense with sheep;* they show that the unrestricted competition of the wools of the southern hemisphere, which is extinguishing the fine-woolled flocks of France, is a subject of serious concern to her statesmen ; and they lead us to sincere congratulation that this delicate and difficult question of the just protection of sheep husbandry and the woollen industry has been so wisely resolved by American legislation.

The friends of the commercial treaties had pointed to the actual figures, which showed a large numerical increase in the exports of France. M. Thiers, in reply to this, points out that there is a very important distinction between an increase of numbers and an augmentation of ascending force. The ascending force of the numbers representing French commerce, which before 1860 was 115 per cent, had fallen, since the treaties, to 65 per cent.

" But it is asked (says M. Thiers) how it is possible that French industry, which had shown such prodigies at the Exposition, could not compete with all the world ? It is true that the French industry has a superiority ; but in what ? In articles of luxury. Yes : our workmen are very skilful ; if they have not the patience of the English workmen, they are no less the most intelligent in Europe. Our silk

products are superior to all ; and also our printed cottons and stuffs.
The English, the Swiss, and the Germans borrow our models, and
thus make a considerable saving. Our designs are above all comparison ; our machines are superior to the English machines ; our
irons, at least before the ruin of the charcoal iron forges, were excellent ; our grains are, at least, as good as those of Arragon and
Naples. But in one thing we are wanting, — cheapness of production :
we have perfection, but we do not have cheapness. Moreover, we
do not have the immense outlets of England ; we have not India and
Australia ; we have not been able to take in all the markets of the
world, the ascendency given by cheapness carried to such a point as
to discourage all rivals. We produce 1,000,000 tons of iron ; England produces 10,000,000 tons ; how can we produce at the same
price ?

"To desire us to enter into rivalry with England in cheapness, is to
mistake the genius of France and the truth of our situation. And
now shall France complain that she cannot supply so many nations
as England? No. She must understand that all nations cannot be
great in the same way. England is the nation of cheap production,
and she must seek after cheap production. This is her career. France
must seek after perfection, and the elevation of her products. How
has she made her fortune in the world, and reached this ascending
force, of which I have so often spoken? Is it by entering into competition with England in the low price of products? No, gentlemen.
It is by selling her silks and printed goods, which have no rivals in
the world. It is by her merinos, it is by her wines, — not the common wines, but the delicate wines, so superior that we made our fortune out of them before the treaties.

"Since the new system, the quality of products of all industries
has been lowered in France. Have our workmen become less skilful? No. But we have sought to rival our neighbors in cheapness.
This is the secret of the situation.

"But this situation is enviable, compared with that of the great and
admirable nation which we call England. God forbid that I should
utter one injurious word against a nation which has been an inviolable
asylum for the proscribed of all revolutions ! — against that nation
which has given us the most beautiful model of human liberty, and
where the government, kept at an equal distance from the passions of
the low and the passions of the high, is to my eyes the ideal of govern-
ments. But I may be allowed to say that it has in its industrial
greatness that which is not so solid as the situation of France.

" France has her consumers within itself. Its market does not depend upon a cannon-shot fired in Europe. And for exportation she has her beautiful products. England, on the contrary, has an artificial existence. She depends upon the doings of the United States; upon the doings of her colonies, which already oppose her with hostile tariffs. May not the day come when its immense production will find no purchasers? She produces ten times as much as her consumption! This little island, in the words of Fox, embraces the world. True; but when she embraces the world, she is vulnerable everywhere.

"Such was the situation of Holland in the seventeenth century, which had realized a prodigy almost as marvellous. What was needed to make Holland, which gave laws to France, to descend from this lofty place? It needed only fifty years. It needed only a Navigation Act in England; it needed only a Colbert in France.

"God forbid that I should predict for England such a destiny ; but, I repeat it, her existence, which depends upon consumers, which she seeks everywhere without herself, is less solid than that of France, which has her consumers in her own bosom.

"I ardently desire that England should continue her career ; but I do not envy that career for our own country. That our country should have her career as brilliant, depends upon your wisdom. It is for you to choose between doctrines puerile and full of illusions, and the doctrines of your old national good sense."

On the 26th of January M. Thiers resumed the discussion of the Economical question before the Assembly, repeating and reinforcing his positions, and replying to objections. We shall limit ourselves to two extracts of general application from the second discourse. The objection so often made by free traders here, that the old industries, which cannot sustain themselves without defensive duties, deserve no protection, is thus vigorously answered : —

"You say that no protection is due to an industry which demands an exaggerated protection, and an eternal protection. That is your principle ; that is the principle of free trade. Let us apply it to France, and come to the bottom of the doctrine.

"Cotton has been protected ever since it came into Europe. It has been protected by prohibition. I repeat that I condemn prohibition ; but I observe that cotton has been protected since the commencement of the eighteenth century, a protection of a hundred years. But you have declared that you would not have an eternal protection. You must then cease to protect cotton, or your maxim is false.

"Wool has been protected since the time of Colbert, and it still demands to be protected. Must we, then, abandon our woollens to the competition of Germans, Belgians, and English? The linen industry has been protected since all time. It ought then, since it has need of permanent protection, to be given up like the others. Iron has been protected since a very ancient period, and still cannot get along without protection. It deserves it no longer, since you admit only temporary protection.

"Our agriculture has been always protected. It still cannot produce grain at the same price as the Crimea, and the plains of Western America. It deserves to be no longer protected. What, then, shall France do? If you dare maintain that she can make cotton cloth at the price of England, woollens at the price of Germany and Belgium, if our metallurgy can contend with that of England, and our agriculture afford grain as cheap as the Crimea and America, then I will acknowledge that there is no longer need of protection ; and thus, all the world being ruined, there will result universal prosperity. I ask again, Can our agriculture produce at the price of the Crimea? (A member, Yes.)

"My adversary proves that he has studied the question more in books than in practice. You can never prove to me that France, with the imposts which weigh upon her agriculture, can produce grain as cheaply as the Crimea.

"What, then, shall we do ? Shall we renounce all our industries, and make only wine? Recall the lessons of history? If there is a country which could content itself with its wines, it is Portugal. What has she become? If France should renounce her industries, her cottons, her woollens, her irons, would not the world say that she had sunk into idiocy ?"

Let those who assert that protective duties are oppressive taxes, imposed upon the mass of the community for the benefit of a monopolist, see how firmly this great practical philosopher plants himself upon the doctrine that protection is a boon to the consumer : —

"It is urged that all the protections accorded to industry constitute monopolies, and that, to enrich a few monopolists, we burden the whole country. It is true there is a monopoly; but it is not in France, it is abroad. I desire to say that this little monopoly, which you accord to French industry, destroys the monopoly of foreign industry.

"When England and France alone worked up cotton, as you know, what was the price of a kilogram of cotton yarn which is now worth three francs? It was worth twenty-seven francs. It is true that this was at the period of our wars, and when the raw material bore a high price; but after the peace the price was still as high as fourteen francs.

"It has gone down now to three francs. And here is the reason why. In proportion as the French production was developed, there was, in spite of prohibition, a sort of penetration between the two markets. We created a competition with England, and thus the cotton fell to three francs.

"What purpose, then, has the monopoly served? It has compelled the foreigner to lower his prices. Every time that you give a protection to a national product, you cause the price of the foreign product to be lowered, and you prevent monopoly.

"Another example more recent. When the linen industry was destroyed in France by the English production by power, a kilogram of thread was worth seven francs. We protected the linen industry in France. This protection permitted competition; and the French product compelled the English manufacturers to lower their prices to three francs fifty centimes.

"If, then, there is any thing evident, it is that this pretended monopoly, this sacrifice of a few centimes, produces a general lowering of price, which is for the benefit of the whole country . . . If you are not willing that the French manufacturers should fabricate, because you have to pay twenty per cent more than in England, it will end in the English making you pay a hundred per cent more.

"If England were the only country to produce certain objects, could you have them at the same price? Certainly not. It is competition, sustained by a just protection, which destroys foreign monopoly. Those who speak of universal, unrestricted competition, do not comprehend it. Do you know what true competition is? It is that no nation should ever suffer itself to make any surrender of its native industries. It is that no one should say that it will no longer manufacture cotton, because it cannot produce as cheaply as another; that no one shall say that it will no longer fabricate cloths, because it cannot fabricate at so good an account as its neighbor; that no one should say that it will not raise grain, under the pretext that grain is pro-

7

duced more dearly than in other countries. The nation which should reason thus would exhibit the reasoning of an idiot. Do you know what is the true competition of nation with nation, the universal competition? It is a noble ambition on the part of each people, — *the noble emulation of producing every thing*, and even that which it produces with less advantage than other people. This competition has, as its result, the reduction of prices to the lowest attainable standard, throughout the entire world."

SIR WENTWORTH DILKE AND THE BRITISH COLONIES.

Our readers cannot fail to be interested by the full extract which we give below, from the English author to whom M. Thiers refers. The work of Sir Wentworth Dilke, "Greater Britain," has attracted much attention in England. The author is a baronet, a member of Parliament, a graduate of Cambridge, a barrister, and a radical in his political opinions. His sentiment for this country is sufficiently shown by the remark that the United States, in the late war, "struck the noblest blow for freedom that the world has ever seen." This article completes the circuit in our review of "The Protective Question Abroad."

"PROTECTION.

"The greatest of all democratic stumbling-blocks is said to be protection.

"'Encourage native industry!' the colonial shop-keeper writes up; 'Show your patriotism, and buy colonial goods!' is painted in huge letters on a shop-front at Castlemaine.

"In England some unscrupulous traders, we are told, write 'From Paris' over their English goods; but such dishonesty in Victoria takes another shape. There we have 'warranted colonial made' placed over imported wares; for many will pay a higher price for a colonial product, confessedly not more than equal to the foreign, such is the rage for native industry, and the hatred of the 'Antipodean doctrine of Free Trade.'

"Many former colonists who lived at home persuaded themselves, and unfortunately persuaded also the public in England, that the protectionists are weak in the colonies. So far is this from being the case in either Victoria or New South Wales, that in the former colony

I found that, in the Lower House, the Free Traders formed but three-elevenths of the Assembly ; and in New South Wales the pastoral tenants of the Crown may be said to stand alone in their support of free trade. Some of the squatters go so far as to declare that none of the public men of the colonies really believe in the advantages of protection ; but that they dishonestly accept the principle, and undertake to act upon it when in office, in order to secure the votes of an ignorant majority of laborers, who are themselves convinced that protection means high wages.

" It would seem as though we free traders had become nearly as bigoted in favor of free trade as our former opponents were in favor of protection. Just as they used to say, We are right : why argue the question ? so now, in face of the support of protection by all the greatest minds in America, all the first statesmen of the Australians, we tell the New England and the Australian politicians that we will not discuss protection with them, because there can be no two minds about it among men of intelligence and education. We will hear no defence of ' national lunacy,' we say.

" If, putting aside our prejudices, we consent to argue with an Australian or American protectionist, we find ourselves in difficulties. All the ordinary arguments, against the compelling people by Act of Parliament to consume a dearer or inferior article, are admitted as soon as they are urged.

" If you attempt to prove that protection is bolstered up by those whose private interests it subserves, you are shown the shrewd Australian diggers, and the calculating Western farmers in America, — men whose pocket interests are wholly opposed to protection, and who yet, almost to a man, support it. A digger at Ballarat defended protection to me in this way : he said he knew that under a protective tariff he had to pay dearer than would otherwise be the case for his jacket and his moleskin trousers, but that he preferred to do this, as, by so doing, he aided in building up in the colony such trades as the making up of clothes, in which his brother, and other men, physically too weak to be diggers, could gain an honest living. In short, the self-denying protection of the Australian diggers is of the character of that which would be accorded to the glaziers of a town by the citizens, if they broke their windows to find their fellow-townsmen work. ' We know we lose, but men must live,' they say. At the same time, they deny that the loss will be enduring. The digger tells you that he should not mind a continuing pocket loss, but that, as a matter of fact, this, which in an old country would be pocket loss, in a new country such as his only comes to this,—that it forms a check on immigration. Wages being five shillings a day in Victoria and three shillings a day in England, workmen would naturally flock into Victoria from England, until wages in Melbourne fell to three shillings sixpence, or four shillings. Here comes in prohibition, and by increasing the cost of living in Victoria, and cutting into the Australian handicraftsman's margin of luxuries, diminishes the temptation to immigration, and consequently the influx itself.

"The Western farmers in America, I have heard, defended protection upon far wider grounds: they admit that free trade would conduce to the most rapid possible peopling of their country with foreign immigrants; but this, they say, is an eminently undesirable conclusion. They prefer to pay a heavy tax in the increased price of every thing they consume, and in the greater cost of labor, rather than see their country demoralized by a rush of Irish or Germans, or their political institutions endangered by a still further increase in the size and power of New York. One old fellow said to me : ' I don't want the Americans in 1900 to be two hundred millions, but I want them to be happy.'

"The American protectionists point to the danger that their countrymen would run, unless town kept pace with country population.

"Settlers would pour off to the West, and drain the juices of the fertile land by cropping it year after year, without fallow, without manure; and then, as the land became in a few years exhausted, would have nowhere whither to turn to find the fertilizers which the soil would need. Were they to depend upon agriculture alone, they would sweep in a wave across the land, leaving behind them a worn-out, depopulated, jungle-covered soil, open to future settlement when its lands should have recovered their fertility by some other and more provident race. The coast lands of the most ancient countries are exhausted, densely bushed, and uninhabited. In this fact lies the power of our sailor race: crossing the seas, we occupy the coasts, and step by step work our way into the upper country, where we should not have attempted to show ourselves had the ancient population resisted us upon the shores. In India, in Ceylon, we met the hardy race of the highlands and interior, only after we had already fixed ourselves upon the coast, with a safe basis for our supply. The fate that these countries have met is that which colonists expect to be their own, unless the protective system be carried out in its entirety. In like manner the Americans point to the ruin of Virginia, and, if you urge ' slavery, answer, ' Slavery is but agriculture.'

" Those who speak of the selfishness of the protectionists as a whole, can never have taken the trouble to examine into the arguments by which protection is supported in Australia and America. In these countries, protection is no mere national delusion : it is a system deliberately adopted with open eyes as one conducive to the country's welfare, in spite of objections known to all, in spite of pocket losses that come home to all. If it be, as we in England believe, a folly, it is at all events a sublime one, full of self-sacrifice, illustrative of a certain nobility in the national heart. The Australian diggers, and Western farmers in America, are setting a grand example to the world of self-sacrifice for a national object; hundreds and thousands of rough men are content to live — they and their families — upon less than they might otherwise enjoy, in order that the condition of the mass of their countrymen may continue raised above that of their brother toilers in Old England.

" Their manufactures are beginning now to stand alone ; but hitherto, without protection, the Americans would have had no cities but seaports. By picturing to ourselves England dependent upon the city of London, upon Liverpool, and Hull, and Bristol, we shall see the necessity the Western men are now under of setting off Pittsburg against New York and Philadelphia. In short, the tendency, according to the Western farmers, of free trade, in the early stages of a country's existence, is to promote universal centralization, to destroy local centres and the commerce they create, to so tax the farmer with the cost of transport to distant markets, that he must grow wheat and corn continuously, and cannot but exhaust his soil. With markets so distant, the richest forest lands are not worth clearing ; and settlements sweep over the country, occupying the poorer lands, and then abandoning them once more.

" Protection in the colonies and America is, to a great degree, a revolt against steam. Steam is making the world all one ; steam ' corrects ' differences in the price of labor. When steam brings all races into competition with each other, the cheaper races will extinguish the dearer, till at last some one people will inhabit the whole earth.

" Coal remains the only power, as it will probably always be cheaper to carry the manufactured goods than to carry the coal.

" Time after time, I have heard the Western farmers draw imaginary pictures of the state of America, if free trade should gain the day, and ask of what avail it is to say that free trade and free circulation of people are profitable to the pocket, if they destroy the national existence of America ; what good to point out the gain of weight to their purses, in the face of the destruction of their religion, their language, and their Saxon institutions?

" One of the greatest of the thinkers of America defended protection to me on the following grounds: That, without protection, America could, at present, have but few and limited manufactures ; — that a nation cannot properly be said to exist as such, unless she has manufactures of many kinds ; for men are born, some with a turn to agriculture, some with a turn to mechanics ; and if you force the mechanic by nature to become a farmer, he will make a bad farmer, and the nation will lose the advantage of his power and invention ; — that the whole of the possible employments of the human race are, in a measure, necessary employments ; necessary to the making up of a nation : — that every concession to free trade cuts out of all chance of action some of the faculties of the American national mind, and, in so doing, weakens and debases it ; — that each and every class of workers is of such importance to the country, that we must make any sacrifice necessary to maintain them in full work : ' The national mind is manifold,' he said ; ' and if you do not keep up every branch of employment, in every district, you waste the national force.'

" If we were to remain a purely agricultural people, land would fall into fewer and fewer hands, and our people become more and more brutalized as the years rolled on.

" It must not be supposed that protection is entirely defended upon these strange new grounds. ' Save us from the pauper-labor of Europe,' is the most recent, as well as the oldest, of protectionist cries. The Australians and Americans say, that by working women at one shilling a day in the mines in Wales, and by generally degrading all laborers under the rank of highly skilled artisans, the British keep wages so low, that, in spite of the cost of carriage, they can almost invariably undersell the colonists and Americans in American and Australian markets. This state of degradation and poverty nothing can force them to introduce into their own countries ; and, on the other hand, they consider manufactures necessary for the national purpose alluded to before. The alternative is protection.

The most unavoidable of all these difficulties of protection — namely, that no human government can ever be trusted to adjust protective taxation without corruption — is no objection to the prohibition which the Western protectionists demand. The New-Englanders say, ' Let us meet the English on fair terms ;' the Western men say that they will not meet them at all. Some of the New York protectionists

declare that their object is merely the fostering of American manufactures until they are able to stand alone, the United States not
having at present reached the point which has been attained by other
nations when they threw protection to the winds. Such halting
protectionists as these manufacturers find no sympathy in Australia
or the West; although the highest of all protectionists look forward to
the distant time when, local centres being everywhere established,
customs will be abolished on all sides, and mankind form one family.
It is a common doctrine in the colonies of England, that a nation cannot be called 'independent' if it has to cry out to another for supplies of necessaries; that true national existence is first attained when
the country becomes capable of supplying to its own citizens those
goods without which they cannot exist in the state of comfort which
they have already reached. Political is apt to follow upon commercial dependency, they say.

"The question of protection is bound up with the wider one of
whether we are to love our fellow-subjects, our race, or the world at
large; whether we are to pursue our country's good at the expense of
other nations. There is a growing belief in England that the noblest
philosophy is to deny the existence of the moral right to benefit ourselves by harming others; that love of mankind must, in time, replace love of race, as that has, in part, replaced narrow patriotism
and love of self. It would seem that our free-trade system lends
itself better to these wide modern sympathies, than does protection.
On the other hand, it may be argued that, if every state consults the
good of its own citizens, we shall, by the action of all nations,
obtain the desired happiness of the whole world, and this with
rapidity.

"The chief thing to be borne in mind in discussing protection with
an Australian or an American is, that he never thinks of denying that,
under protection, he pays a higher price for his goods than he would
if he bought them from us; and that he admits at once that he temporarily pays a tax of fifteen or twenty per cent upon every thing he
buys, in order to help set his country on the road to national unity
and ultimate wealth. Without protection, the American tells you,
there will be commercial New York, sugar-growing Louisiana, the
corn-growing North-west, but no America: protection alone can
give him a united country. When we talk about things being to the
advantage or disadvantage of a country, the American protectionist
asks what you mean. Admitting that all you say against protection
may be true, he says that he had sooner see America supporting a

hundred millions independent of the remainder of the world, than two
hundred millions dependent for clothes upon the British. ' You, on
the other hand,' he says, ' would prefer our custom.' How can we
discuss this question? The difference between us is radical, and we
have no base on which to build, from the reason that every country
understands its own interests better than it does those of its neighbor.
As a rule, the colonists hold that they should not protect themselves
against the sister colonies, but only against the outer world; and
while I was in Melbourne, an arrangement was made with respect
to the broader customs between Victoria and New South Wales; but
this is at present the only step that has been taken towards inter-
colonial free trade.

"It is passing strange that Victoria should be noted for the eagerness with which her people seek protection. Possessed of little coal,
they appear to be attempting artificially to create an industry which,
owing to this sad lack of fuel, must languish from the moment that it is
let alone. Sydney coal sells in Melbourne at thirty shillings a ton;
at the pit's mouth, at Newcastle, New South Wales, it fetches only
seven or eight shillings. With regard, however, to the making-up of
native produce, the question in the case of Victoria is merely this: Is
it cheaper to carry the wool to the coal, and then the woollen goods
back again, than to carry the coal to the wool? And as long as
Victoria can continue to export wheat, so that the coal ships may not
want freight, wool manufacturers may prosper in Victoria.

"The Victorians naturally deny that the cost of coal has much to
do with the question. The French manufactures, they point out,
with dearer coal, but with cheaper labor, have in many branches of
trade beaten the English out of common markets; but, then, under
protection, there is no chance of cheap labor in Victoria.

"Writing for the Englishmen of Old England, it is not necessary
for me to defend free trade by any arguments. As far as we in our
island are concerned, it is so manifestly to the pocket interest of
almost all of us, and at the same time, on account of the minuteness
of our territory, so little dangerous politically, that for Britain there
can be no danger of a deliberate relapse into protection; although we
have but little right to talk about free trade, so long as we continue
our enormous subsidies to the Cunard liners.

"The American argument in favor of prohibition is, in the main,
it will be seen, political; the economical objections being admitted,
but outweighed. Our action in the matter of our postal contracts,
and in the case of the Factory Acts, at all events shows that we are

not ourselves invariably averse to distinguish between the political and the economical aspect of certain questions.

"My duty has been to chronicle what is said and thought upon the matter in our various plantations. One thing, at least, is clear, that even if the opinions I have recorded be as ridiculous when applied to Australia or America as they would be when applied to England, they are not supported by a selfish clique, but rest upon the generosity and self-sacrifice of a majority of the population."

REMARKS AT THE INDIANAPOLIS EXPOSITION, AUG. 2, 1870, BY JOHN L. HAYES.*

Mr. President, Ladies and Gentlemen, — I intend to confine my remarks entirely to the subject of the woollen manufacture, and topics connected with it. The protective system which was established by our fathers, — for the protective system was established by the first Act which was passed by Congress after the inauguration of our government, — and which has been continued with more or less efficiency during the whole period of our national history, had placed our woollen industry, at the time of our great war, in a position to do its part in providing the industrial resources and the means necessary for carrying on the war. That war was one in which victory was won by the North, not by its skill, not by its courage, not by its military genius, not by its patriotism; but it was really won through the industrial resources of the North. It was won because the North had power — industrial power; because it had strength — material strength, growing out of its diversified industry.

I say the woollen industry of this country, at the period of the war, was in a position to perform its part; it did perform a very important part throughout the war. Our mills, our looms, and our sewing machines used up no less than two hundred millions pounds of wool during the war, for the benefit of the army and navy. In one single year of the war we furnished thirty-five millions of garments to our soldiers. Our army was better clothed than any other army ever was in the history of the world. They were clothed in wool — in sound cloths; and the Quarter-Master-General of the Army has officially reported that there is no army upon earth so well clothed as that of the United States, or as it was clothed during the war.

But the clothing of our army and navy, and the furnishing of the industrial resources necessary to the nation, in its time of difficulty, is not the only good result of our woollen industry. Some persons are disposed to speak slightingly, and even sneeringly, of the clothing interest; for the growing of wool, the making of woollens, and the conversion of them into garments constitutes but one

---

* These remarks, made wholly without notes, were originally reported in the "Indianapolis Journal." The editor, in reproducing them, follows substantially the original report, supplying omissions of quotations, and correcting some statements and figures imperfectly understood by the reporter.

great interest. The great British author, Thomas Carlyle, has written a work which he calls *Sartor Resartus,* or "The Tailor Sewed Over." This work he characterizes as the "philosophy of clothes," and takes this subject as the vehicle of his satire upon the subject of mere externals. He says that in turning a corner in the Scottish town of Edinburgh he came upon a sign on which was written So-and-so, "Breeches-maker to His Majesty;" and then followed the words *sic itur ad astra,*—"so we ascend to the stars." This was intended as satire; but there was a great deal more truth in it than the philosopher conceived of. The prime necessities of the whole world of mankind consists of a very few things,—food, clothing, and the means of shelter. Clothing is one of the first great essentials of man. Take, if you please, your household expenses, and see what they indicate as to the importance of this class of commodities. You will find, that, in the necessary expenses of the family, clothing has the second place, always next to the article of food; and in fashionable families, very often the first place of all. What, therefore, can conduce so much to the absolute comfort of the homes and households of the country, as to increase and improve the means of obtaining cheap, good, and substantial clothing? If we are enabled to use double the amount, in value, of clothing, or to get it at one-half the money; or, in other words, if we are enabled for the least possible expenditure of labor to get the largest possible amount of clothing, how much is thereby added to the comfort of the people! That is the grand object of the wool industry of this country.

What is the present position of our woollen manufacture? We consume, in this country, two hundred and forty millions of dollars' worth of woollen manufactures, or of manufactures of which wool is the chief component, per annum. Of that amount we import thirty-two millions of dollars' worth. Of this thirty-two millions about six millions are in cloths; about fifteen millions in dress goods; about two millions in carpets of certain classes. But when we say we import thirty-two millions, bear in mind that that is the declared value,—the amount on which the duty is paid; we have got to add to that the cost of the duties and the charges or profits of the importer, which will double it; so that we may put the total value of our imports at sixty-four millions of dollars. Estimates, very carefully made, show that we produced, in the year 1868, one hundred and seventy-five millions dollars' worth of woollen manufactures; adding to what we produced ourselves what we imported, we consume, in round numbers, two hundred and forty millions. And we may safely say, that we produce here, of our own manufacture, nearly three-fourths of all the woollen goods used in this country.

But when we come to look at it practically, we find that for the goods consumed by the great masses of the people, we are very largely independent of all foreign countries. A few years ago all the materials used for our great coats, such as beaver and Esquimaux cloths, were made abroad; but, within the last five years, we have succeeded in making those goods of an excellent quality at home; and, practically, we now make all the cloths that we use for our great coats. We make all our under-goods, stockings, hosiery, and goods for under-clothing, amounting to some forty millions of dollars. Three or four years ago we made no goods of the class that are made fitted to the form; but within two or three years past we have succeeded in making these also, not by hand, but by machinery, and surpassing in quality any goods of the kind that are made abroad. And the result of this has been, that American competition has actually reduced the prices of the foreign articles at least six dollars on the dozen.

Then we have introduced, within the last five or six years, a very large class of dress goods. During the war there was an association of patriotic ladies formed, who pledged themselves that they would not wear any thing but American goods. But when these patriotic ladies went into the shops to make their purchases, they found, to their great mortification, that there was a sad deficiency in the better classes of dress goods of American manufacture. But it is not so now. Now the ladies can be dressed, and most elegantly dressed, in American goods entirely. The silk goods that were shown in the Exposition at New York compared favorably with any that are made abroad. Our silks, our lustres, our serges, and a great variety of cotton stuffs, of a class not made in this country at all, until within the last five years, challenge comparison with any similar articles made abroad. And in the article of carpets, I say, without hesitation, that we surpass the manufacturers of any other country on the globe. We can make, at this very time, all the ingrain, two-ply, and three-ply carpets that are used in this country. We have nearly twice the number of looms engaged in that branch of manufacture that are to be found in England; and our carpets are so far superior to those of English manufacture, that there are now, comparatively, none at all of that class of carpets imported into this country. The materials of which the English carpets of that class are made are so poor and weak that they cannot be woven by power looms, but have to be made by hand looms; while ours are made in the power loom, are of better and stronger materials, and superior in every respect.

Of the Brussels and other rich and expensive carpets, nearly one-half are made in this country. Within the last two years we have succeeded in manufacturing what is known as the Axminster carpet. That is a carpet which is laid down in palaces, — a carpet that costs eight dollars a yard. These carpets are made in Europe by hand; but we have been able to make them by the power loom, superior in strength to the French, and in beauty and finish so exact a copy of the originals that, if you lay the two side by side, you cannot tell them apart. And these we make at so low a cost, that we have compelled the manufacturer of the foreign article to reduce his price a dollar or two a yard, although the American Axminsters are frequently put upon the market and sold for the imported article.

Your own Exposition shows how much you have done; but the great fact to be looked at is, that we have not only done all this, but that we have been enabled to make these goods cheaper through the competition that grows out of our protective system. Our import duties are the great barrier that prevents the influx of the great tide of foreign importation that would otherwise sweep over us. If you will take the pains to compare the prices of goods at the present time with the prices that prevailed in 1860, just before the war, and before the present tariff was levied, you will see what has been the result of the protective system. Now you cannot ordinarily arrive at a satisfactory comparison of prices of cloths at periods so far apart, for the reason that there will be some difference in style, finish, coloring, or in some other respect, between any two pieces manufactured ten years apart. You must have an uniform standard; and the only such standard you can have is the article of flannel; and every piece of cloth at one stage of its manufacture is a piece of flannel. That, therefore, we take as a standard in a comparison of the prices of 1860 and those of the present year. We have careful and accurate reports from two of the first flannel commercial houses in the United States, engaged in the selling of flannels, houses which represent the sales of twenty different establishments, and the products of at least one hundred different sets of machinery. That report shows, in one house, that the prices in gold at which their flannels sell at the present time are twenty-one per cent less than they were in 1860, and in the other establishment sixteen per cent less. The fact is there demonstrated by the prices of flannels, which are an uniform standard ; it is settled beyond contradiction how much the country has gained by this protective system, and the competition which grows out of it.

I say, therefore, as a result of the tariff and the protective system, that prices are much lower to the consumer. I will go further, and say that for the wool-grower, who sells his product to the factory alongside of him, the prices of woollen clothing at the present time are at least fifty per cent lower than before the war; and before the woollen mills were established in your midst, through the protection afforded by the Morrill tariff and the tariff of 1867.

Now, what is the one great power by which we are enabled to clothe the masses of our people with a hundred and seventy-five millions dollars' worth of goods of home manufacture ? I answer, It is the possession, mainly, of an animal which some persons are accustomed to regard with contempt, and which John Randolph, of Roanoke, once said he would always go out of his way to kick, — and that is the sheep ; and more than all is it owing to the fact that this country has the possession of the merino sheep. Here we have an illustration of the connection and mutual relation of agriculture and manufactures ; and the historical facts, which I shall now briefly review, will show how absolutely the manufacturing interests of this as well as every other country are dependent upon its agriculture.

The Romans wore nothing but woollen goods. They had no cotton ; they had a little linen which was worn as a material of luxury; they had no silk. They cultivated the sheep with great care, and some of their richest possessions were in sheep. But there was one breed of sheep which they cultivated with extraordinary care, and by that system of selection which Darwin speaks of as the source of the perfected forms of our domestic animals. It was called the Tarentine sheep, from Tarentum, a city of Greek origin, situated at the head of the Tarentine gulf. The fleece of this sheep was of exceeding fineness ; it was of great delicacy, and the prices of its fleeces were enormous. The sheep were clothed in cold weather to keep them warm; and the result was that they were very tender and their wool was very fine. They were a product of Greek civilization transmitted down to the Romans. Columella, the great Roman agriculturist, says that his uncle, residing in Spain, crossed some of the fine Tarentine sheep with some rams that had been imported from Africa; and the consequence was, that these animals had the whiteness of the father with the fineness of the fleece of the mother, and that that race was perpetuated. Here we see an improvement of the stock, — an increase of strength and productiveness given to the fine-wool sheep of Spain. At that time the sheep of Spain were of immense value; for Strabo says that sheep from Spain, in the time of Tiberius, were carried to Rome, and sold for the price of a *talent*, one thousand dollars a head. In the time of our Saviour a thousand dollars was given in Rome for a Spanish sheep. When the barbarians inundated Italy, these fine-wool sheep were all swept away, but they remained in Spain ; they were cultivated by the Moors in the mountains of Spain, which were almost inaccessible, and were not reached by the hordes of Huns, and other Northern barbarians, which had laid waste the greater portion of the Roman possessions. They continued to be nourished there by the Moors, who were very much advanced in arts; and further on were found there as the Spanish merino. So that the Spanish merino which we now have, if not the only, is at all events by far the most important relic that we have to-day which has come down to us from Greek and Roman material civilization. We have here a direct inheritance from the material wealth of the Old World civilization.

What was the result of the possession of this race of animals to the countries which could command their fleeces? The Moors, before their expulsion from Spain, had 16,000 looms employed in making the fine cloths then known. The States of Italy, in the twelfth and thirteenth centuries, established commerce on the ancient routes of navigation to the East. They made the Spanish wool, which they secured by their commerce, into fine cloths; and we find that Florence, Genoa, Pisa, and Venice acquired their wealth and splendor, and the material of their commerce, from the woollen manufacture. The arts flourished as wealth increased; and we find the colossal statue of David, one of the grandest works of the great Michel Angelo, purchased by the Wool-Workers' Guild.

The arts declined in Italy. They then went over to the low countries, — the Netherlands. The Netherlands were in possession of this Spanish fleece, from the fact that the two monarchies had been combined under King Charles the Fifth. Their precious cloths were carried all over the East, and all over the world which was then known. From the Netherlands the wool manufacture was carried to England, to Germany, and to France. Such was the early result of the possession of this animal, and of the wool manufacture which this animal supplied.

It was scarcely one century ago that Western Europe determined to get possesion of this merino race. The King of Saxony sent out to Spain to get it in 1776. At that time, of such importance was the culture of this animal held to be, that the mode of cultivating them was directed to be read before the service in the churches on Sunday. What is the result of that importation? We have now the Saxony sheep with fleeces vastly fiuer than the old Spanish stock. The King of Prussia, Frederick the Second, introduced about three hundred of these sheep into his kingdom, and persevered in their culture until they were established in Prussia. What is the result of that? Eighteen per cent of all Prussian exports now are fine woollen goods from the merino sheep. The great Maria Theresa, in 1776, introduced the merino sheep into Hungary, and established them there. At this time the finest manufacture of Hungary is her cloth, and the most valuable of all her possessions are her flocks. Louis the Sixteenth, in 1786, introduced the merino sheep into France. The great Colbert, a century before that, had endeavored to establish it there, and failed. But Daubenton, the great naturalist, and the associate of Buffon, had made the sheep a subject of study, and with his assistance the merino race was established in that country. The result is, that France to-day has the finest manufactures in the world, only a century after the introduction of the Spanish sheep into that country. The stock of sheep of Rambouillet still exists. Said Napoleon: "Spain has twenty-five millions of merinos; France shall have one hundred millions;" and he established three hundred sheep-folds all over France. One of the most interesting and most touching incidents, as showing the interest which the great people of the world have in the culture of this animal, is this: The sheep-fold of

Rambouillet was about to be destroyed. The Empress Eugenie, the wife of the present Emperor, learned that such was the fact, and she at once declared that it should not be done, — that the Rambouillet sheep-fold was identified with the industrial prosperity of France ; and she took the flock of Rambouillet under her special protection, declaring that it should be regarded as her personal charge.

Thus we find all the continent of Europe provided with this race of sheep less than a century ago. A little later, about the commencement of the present century, the merinos were introduced into this country. The best family of our merinos came from an importation which we owe, indirectly, to George Washington. For Colonel Humphreys — who had been an aid of Washington, and who had been stimulated by Washington with that love of agriculture which was so strong a feature in his character — having been appointed minister to Spain, brought home with him, in 1802, the most important of the early importations of the merino sheep, which had been selected from the best Spanish families. From this Humphreys's sheep have come our American merinos, a peculiar breed, and one of the finest in the world.*

I may say in regard to the improvement which has been made in this country in the culture of sheep, that our American merinos, our best improved American sheep, produced more washed wool in 1846 than they did of unwashed wool when first introduced ; and that they now produce twice the amount of scoured wool that the original Spanish sheep did. It is one of the most productive sheep in the world. I may say that the possession of the merino fleece, which composes now a great proportion of the fleece of this country, is to fabrics precisely what wheat and flour are to grain. We may eat corn bread and rye bread occasionally, for a change ; but we all, in the long-run, have to come back to wheat. So it is with merino wool ; it is the great foundation of all fabrics. Its fibre is finer than any other. The greater the number of strands there are in a wire cable, the stronger it is ; and just so, the greater the number of fibres that are contained in a yarn of a given diameter, the greater will be its strength. Merino wool constitutes the greatest portion of the cloths of the world ; it is the wool of which there is the highest necessity.

I am coming now to my point (and I fear you may think I am a long time in coming to it). My point is this : Our merino wool culture was at one time on the point of being destroyed by the immense increase of the wool product of South American countries, — La Plata and Buenos Ayres. The increase within seven years was, in La Plata alone, from sixteen millions to fifty-nine millions of pounds per annum. The wool-growers and the wool manufacturers came together. There was at that time no division or classification of the grades of wool with respect to the tariff duty, except upon the basis of the price ; and there was always an opportunity to bring in the wool a little dirtier, and in that manner avoid the proper duty. Instead of six cents per pound, the proper duty, the importers of wool and manufacturers paid practically but three cents. The wool-growers demanded an increase on the duties on wool ; the wool manufacturers assented. The wool duty upon the great bulk of imported wools was increased from an average of about three cents up to ten cents specific, and eleven cents

* In the speech, as delivered and reported, it was inaccurately stated that the Humphreys's merinos were the first ever brought to America which actually survived. This error, which is now corrected, was kindly pointed out, in a private letter, by Dr. Randall.

ad valorem; and the result was simply the salvation of the growth of wool in this country. The fine wool husbandry in the Southern Hemisphere had grown so rapidly, from the failure of the cotton crops of this country, that when the war closed, if it had not been for this wool tariff, there would have been such an importation from the Southern Hemisphere as would have wiped out the merino flocks of this country, — one of the most important of our material resources. The wool tariff saved it. Before the tariff was applied, the importation of wool from Buenos Ayres and the Cape of Good Hope was thirty-six thousand bales; in the next year, after the woollen tariff went into operation, the importations were only about seven thousand bales; so that there was actually a relief to the wool-growers of this country, from the ruinous competition, of thirty thousand bales of foreign wool. Of course I need not tell you that this measure was the salvation of the wool-growing interests of this country.

Nevertheless the manufacturers were much troubled about this tariff. They accepted it at first as a necessity, but yet the demands of the wool-growers for this increased duty proved to be really the salvation of the wool manufacturer. The fair demand of the manufacturer was, that he should be placed in the same position as if he had his wool still free from duty; and accordingly a neutralizing duty was placed upon cloth — fifty cents per pound — to offset the duty of about twelve cents per pound on wool; it taking about four pounds of wool, upon the average, to make a yard of cloth. As the tariff went into operation the wool manufacturer felt its operation first. This fifty cents per pound on cloth was a barrier which was raised against the importation of foreign cloths; and, but for the demands of the wool-grower for protection to his interests, the manufacturer would not have had the benefit of it. The result has been to shut out European goods, and to build up our home manufactures as nothing ever did before. To the demands of the wool-growers we owe the best protection that has ever been given to our manufacturers. Said an intelligent manufacturer to me the other day, "I have been manufacturing wool for thirty years, and this is the first time the plug has ever been in."

Now, if our government has given this encouragement to the woollen manufacture, the next question is, Has the manufacturer responded? Has he done his duty? in other words, has it paid to encourage the manufacturer?

Let us make a comparison between the position of the woollen manufacturer in this country and the industry abroad. And I cannot express my ideas upon this point in a better way than by reading an extract from a report upon woollens, at the Paris Exposition, prepared conjointly by one of the most eminent of our practical manufacturers and myself: —

"A more important point of comparison between American and foreign fabrics is the relative cost of production of such manufactures as we have most successfully achieved here, measured by the only correct standard, the relative expenditure of human labor required for such production. The solution of this question will determine whether we have such natural or acquired advantages as will justify the encouragement of this manufacture as a national industry. In pursuing this inquiry, we can fix upon no single representative article of uniform quality and value; such as a ton of pig iron, the relative cost of which would determine the comparative advantages of the American or foreigner in the manufacture of iron. The infinite variety of cloths forbids the selection of any one as the standard of comparison, even if it were possible to obtain data from the books of foreign manufacturers. This question must be solved for the products of the card-wool industry, generally, by comparing the efficiency of our system, processes, and machinery of fabrication. The many practical manufacturers who have recently visited Europe, for the express purpose of studying its industries, concur in declaring that, in these respects, we are on an equality with the most advanced nations. Laying aside the supposed advantages which we have, in the possession of water-power, upon which far too much stress is laid in popular estimates, we apply every-where, in our fabrication of woollens, the factory system, and make the utmost use of mechanical power, while handicraft processes are still largely used abroad, especially in weaving. For the preparation of card-wool, no machinery at the Exposition equalled in efficiency the American burring machinery exhibited there, such as is in general use here. In the carding of wool no improvements were seen at Verviers, one of the chief centres of the card-wool industry in Europe, which we do not have in use. About the same number of hands were employed at the cards as here. Spinning, in large estab-lishments abroad, is usually performed by mules; while jack spinning is more generally adopted in New England, as better suited to the different qualities and quantities of yarns demanded by the variety of fabrics usually produced in our mills. The mules used here are of equal efficiency with those in the best mills in Europe. With respect to weaving, it was remarked that looms were being constructed at the machine shops at Verviers, such as we would not put into our mills to-day. It was also remarked, that no European looms for weaving fancy goods were shown at the Exposition, which would bear comparison with the Crompton loom, and even upon that admirable machine great improvements are known to be in progress. The other processes of manufacture, such as dyeing, are the same as in Europe. When we take into consideration the greater energy and intelligence of our better fed and better educated workmen; the necessary use of every labor-saving process, on account of the higher cost of labor here; and the admitted superiority in construction of American machinery, — it may be safely asserted that a yard of cloth is made in this country with less hours of human labor than one of equal quality and the same degree of finish abroad. In other words, a week's labor will produce more yards of cloth in an American than in an European mill. But it is said that a yard of cloth costs less in Europe than in the United States. Even this statement requires qualification, for the American laborer can purchase here more yards of cloth, by the produce of a day's work, than the European laborer, the ratio of the price of cloth in this country, to-day, not being in proportion to the ratio of the rate of wages of ordinary labor. It is still true, that the money cost of producing cloths is greater in this country than in Europe. From what has been said, it is apparent that the greater money cost of fabricating cloths is not due to any want of natural advan-tages, or any deficiency in skill and effective labor on the part of the American manu-facturer. It is not true of this industry, as is often asserted by theorists, that it has a sickly and hot-bed growth, sustained only by artificial stimulus; and rendering its pro-ductions as unnatural, to use Adam Smith's often-quoted comparison, 'as that of wine produced from grapes grown in the hot-houses of Scotland.' The higher cost of produc-tion in that country is due, solely, to national causes inherent to the condition of a new country and a progressive people, or the higher rates of interest on capital required to initiate and sustain industrial enterprise, and the higher rates of labor demanded by the greater social and educational requirements of our industrial population."

So we see that the free-trade argument, that unrestricted competition with other nations would lead us to the exercise of higher skill, amounts to nothing at all. We have already in the woollen manufacture more skill than foreign nations; for a week's labor in the American mills produces more than a week's labor in the mills abroad. If we had unrestricted foreign competition with our home products, how should we be able to pay our high prices for labor? How could we keep up the rates of labor to that standard which is essential to the prosperity of our workmen? We protectionists declare, as the foundation of our whole argument, that the wages of labor should be brought up, and kept up ; while, on the other side, they invariably acknowledge, if they are fair and intelligent men, that the results of free trade will be to reduce the price of labor; and that we cannot continue to manufacture and compete with foreigners except by reducing the price of labor to the foreign standard. A certain class of philosophers and benevolent men in this country, and among them a good many of those who have been advocates of free soil doctrines, — such men as William Lloyd Garrison and Wendell Phillips, — carried away by the sentiment of universal philanthropy, have been inclined to the side of free trade, and to overlook entirely the particular interests of this country. But I find, in a very recent letter of Mr. Phillips, some remarks embodying an argument which covers the whole ground upon which we found protection. The blessings of protection and the malign results of free trade were never more eloquently portrayed than in the vivid words which I will read to you : —

" Putting aside all theories, every lover of progress must see with profound regret the introduction here of any element which will lessen wages. The mainspring of our progress is high wages, — wages at such a level that the workingman can spare his wife to preside over a ' home,' can command leisure, go to lectures, take a newspaper, and lift himself from the deadening level of mere toil. That dollar left after all the bills are paid on Saturday night means education, independence, self-respect, manhood : it increases the value of every acre near by, fills the to vn with dwellings, opens public libraries and crowds them ; dots the continent with cities, and cobwebs it with railways. That one remaining dollar insures progress, and guarantees millions to its owner better than a score of stat-utes. It is worth more than a thousand colleges, and makes armies and police superfluous."

I have not talked about the improvement of the woollen manufacture abroad, but here at home, — as applied to this country, — because I conceive that that is what we have to do with. Providence has so arranged it that the instinct of self-preservation shall be the strongest instinct of our nature. In a man of little culture, where that instinct is strong, it leads to selfishness; give him more culture, and it leads to a kind of selfishness, — to self-interest; next, he looks not only at his own personal interests, but at those of his family ; and with a still greater degree of enlightenment and culture he begins to look after his country. When a man goes outside of his country to work, he generally works with very little effect. With the old Greeks and Romans, patriotism was the first of all the virtues ; and during our war we thought patriotism was a very great virtue ; we partook a great deal of the Greek and Roman sentiment on that subject, and our young men were so inspired by that sentiment that they could pour out their life-blood with a smile of peace and triumph. We now hear the tocsin of war resounding through Europe, and we are about to witness there one of those great conflicts which, in the end, are always sure to advance the cause of human liberty. Meanwhile, in this country, we find the Germans, almost as one man, crying out for Fatherland ; and upon the other hand, the French, with one voice, shouting for their country, forgetful of every wrong, forgetful of exile, forgetful of every feeling of animosity toward the Emperor. To them France is still *Ma mère bien aimée*, " My mother well beloved." One of Paradol's last expressions was, " If war breaks out in France, there will be but one party, — the party of the Government."

9

The most sublime example, illustrating this love of country, is that of the great Author of our religion : "O Jerusalem! Jerusalem! How often would I have gathered thy children together as a hen gathereth her brood under her wings." What depth of love for his country was there! I once heard Parodi sing those words to the music of one of the great Masters, and as she prolonged the words, "Jerusalem! Jerusalem!" it brought most vividly before my mind the thought of the agony of love which Jesus had for the country of his fathers. I felt that the doctrine that the love of country must be subordinate to that universal philanthropy which is declared and preached for by free-trade theorists, and men of that class, is the idlest clamor in the world. The human heart and the sentiments of religion declare this. All these things teach us that it is through the development of our own country that we are to carry out the great work which we are called upon to do for the good of mankind. In Expositions like this we are no less truly fighting for our country than if we were fighting for her upon the field of battle. We are doing our part to carry out the country's industrial independence, — the only sure foundation of the prosperity of every nation. And when I hear men preaching free-trade theories, and see Americans accepting and repeating the lessons taught them by England, for the purely selfish purpose of putting down and keeping down our industrial independence, I cannot restrain my indignation. I feel as Jefferson felt towards the Americans of his time who were for assimilating us to the rotten as well as sound parts of the British model, when he described the apostates who had gone over to these heresies as "men who were Samsons in the field and Solomons in the council, but who have had their heads shorn by the harlot England."

Let me say in conclusion, gentlemen, that the intelligent manufacturers of New England rejoice in the progress of manufactures at the West. They know very well that the undeniable effect of competition is to diminish the consumption of Eastern goods. But they know that this competition, which reduces the prices to consumers, is the strongest argument for the protective policy, without which neither the manufacturers of the East or the West could live for a moment. The true work of the East is the higher branches of manufacture, demanding the investment of more capital and the employment of the most skilled labor. Such a field exists in the worsted manufacture, or that of dress goods. Our largest clothing mill has already taken off fifty sets from the manufacture of cloths, and is employing its capital in the production of dress goods.

The only obstacle to that movement is the want of confidence in the continuance of our protective system. It would cost a million or two millions of dollars to build a worsted mill which could fairly compete with the best mills of Bradford or Roubaix. So long as British influence can make it doubtful whether our protective system will continue, American capital will fail to flow into the new investments in the woollen manufacture. The British manufacturers can well afford, therefore, to agitate free trade in this country. They do not expect to repeal our tariff laws, but they deter capital from new manufacturing investments. It is really British influence which is now retarding our national progress, just as it did in the early period of our national existence. It is this influence, which, unconsciously it may be, makes men, who are otherwise honest and patriotic, advocates of the baleful system of British free trade; and which makes the remark of Mr. Jefferson, in his letter to Mr. Mazzei, as true now as it was then.